TEACHING TO MEET

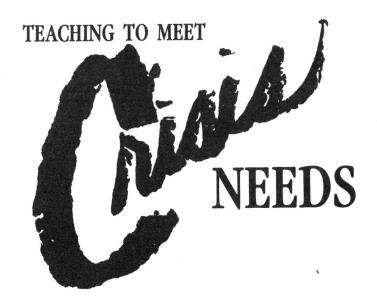

NEEDS

Billie Davis

Gospel Publishing House
Springfield, Missouri
02-0609

This is a Workers Training Division textbook. Credit for its study will
be issued under Classification 4, Sunday School Department, Assemblies of God.

Library of Congress Catalog Card Number 83-82815
International Standard Book Number 0-88243-609-0
Printed in the United States of America

Contents

Introduction

This is a special kind of book designed to help Christian workers meet the needs of people in today's complex world. Almost every television program, newspaper, and magazine makes reference to problems of unhappy homes, adolescent trauma, mid-life crisis, alcohol and drug abuse, difficulties with work and money, illness, death, and grief. Any one of these problems creates crisis. People face crises any time a change occurs in the way their basic needs are met. Racks of books are available on how to cope with these problems. Seminars and classes offering solutions are advertised in the papers and on bulletin boards.

After several years of study in the field of behavioral science (psychology, sociology, counseling, and social work), and seminar attendance, I came to this conclusion: The most helpful ideas used by the best trained experts are basic principles found in the Bible. And the methods of helping people in times of crisis and trouble are very similar to the teaching methods used by Jesus and the apostles. These methods also form the pattern of every good Sunday school class.

The goals of the experts in this field are to help people be happy and productive on earth. Even though these experts are not claiming their work to be a Christian endeavor, the successful ideas and methods they developed are really Biblical principles. Dedicated people in various occupations study to develop technical improvements so they can offer the best possible product. If teachers would develop teaching skills in the same way, what a blessing they could be!

So this book presents some facts and methods related to the

behavioral sciences to help you more effectively meet the needs of troubled and hurting people. Although these are concepts presented in college classes, here they are coupled with some practical suggestions to challenge you to use the Sunday school class situation to meet the needs of your students. You can not only show people the way to live forever in unlimited joy with the Lord, you can also help people to cope with life on earth.

1

Hope Is in the Word

This is my comfort in my affliction: for thy word hath quickened me. . . . I hope in thy word (Psalm 119:50,81, KJV).

Where can people with serious problems go for help? Where can they go for comfort and direction in times of crisis? You are not likely to answer, "To Sunday school, of course!" But the ideal Sunday school class fits almost perfectly the description of a setting where human needs are met and problems can be solved. Let's examine this remarkable idea.

Today there is a general awareness that people are hurting. Christians tend to blame social conditions and impersonal formalized churches for not meeting human needs. Some say the church should provide for more personal interaction and show more genuine love and concern for people in crisis. Others say the church should provide more opportunities for counseling.

This high regard for counseling is based upon the assumption that people need to express their problems and fears in an environment of openness and acceptance. In the preferred counseling situation, confused, distraught persons are encouraged to see their situations in new perspectives. They learn to understand their own feelings. They learn principles that enable them to cope with problems and crises. They develop new attitudes, find new satisfactions, and learn more mature, productive behavior. These are the goals of counseling.

Sunday School and Counseling

Most Sunday school teachers are not counselors in the professional sense, and should not try to be. Yet, they have a ministry that shares some of counseling's goals. In fact, the Sunday school is based upon the same set of values and principles as modern Christian counseling.

This parallelism becomes obvious as we look at both the Sunday school's purpose and its unique contributions to the Christian ministry. Following are some examples of the rationale for making Sunday school a part of the church program.

1. Individuals of various age-groups and life situations have characteristics and needs that require more specific recognition and ministry than the more formal public church service can offer. Sunday school classes facilitate the meeting of this need.

2. In Sunday school, the Word of God is studied and applied to specific life situations.

3. Adults and children need contacts with Christians who are in positions of authority less formal than that of a clergyman. The Sunday school teacher has such a position, and can be looked to for information, wisdom, and understanding.

4. In Sunday school, people have opportunities to ask questions, discuss problems, and receive immediate, specific feedback. People are helped and encourged by peer-group interaction.

5. Sunday school teachers are trained to meet specific needs through appropriate methods and materials. They study human behavior and characteristics so they can be understanding in personal situations. They make personal contacts, visit homes, and become aware of environmental and social factors affecting the feelings and behavior of the students.

6. The Sunday school format and procedures encourage the development of consistent behavior and formation of good habits in that it provides a relatively stable group with relatively consistent expectations.

History of Sunday School

The Sunday school was founded in response to social crisis and human need, Robert Raikes gathering rowdy urchins off the streets of Gloucester, England, and teaching them the Word of God. His purpose was to keep them out of trouble and help them find a better quality of life.

From a class for ragged youngsters, the Sunday school developed into a teaching facility for children of all social levels and ages. Then, in America, with its New World emphasis upon universal education, the Sunday school idea was expanded to include Bible classes for adults. Later, class organization went beyond age groupings to student interests and life situations (e.g., electives). Specialized groups were formed and publishers addressed their materials to teenagers, young married couples, and college and career classes. One of the latest additions to the educational program in many churches is a special department for single members.

The Sunday school rationale and development indicate that Christian leaders have long recognized the value of Bible teaching in meeting the needs of people in various stages and conditions of life. Surely the modern Sunday school teacher has a distinctive role in the church's ministry to people in crisis. The teacher must be prepared by understanding Biblical problem solving techniques.

Human Crisis and Personal Problem Solving

SUNDAY SCHOOL AND CHRISTIAN COUNSELING PRINCIPLES

The same kinds of human needs that provide purpose and rationale for counseling provide purpose and rationale for Christian education. This does not mean that Sunday school teachers are counselors, but that they minister to many of the same kinds of needs that counselors do. The difference is in the approach and procedures. Some people may need the services of professional counselors. Others can find their needs met in the Sunday school class itself. Still others will be kept from developing severe problems as their lives are enriched through Bible teaching.

Our position is not that teachers take the place of counselors, but that good Bible teaching by concerned teachers will contain counseling elements, just as good counseling contains teaching elements. The relationship between teaching and counseling is well established in counseling theory. Lawrence Crabb proposes that the counseling activity is composed of three levels: encouragement, exhortation, and enlightenment. He believes that most Sunday school teachers and other Christian workers are capable of being trained in the first two levels, and that many counseling needs can be met within the church community.[1]

PROCESS OF LEARNING APPLIED TO HANDLING CRISES

To a great extent, personal problem solving and adjustment to crisis situations is a matter of *learning.* People generally perceive and accept the connection between learning and personal problem solving. This is evidenced by the popularity of self-help books. Psychologist Gary Collins, among other scholars in the field, suggests that the self-help movement may indicate a failure of the church to meet personal needs and provide answers to the complex problems of modern society.[2] The popular acceptance in Christian circles of listening to a well-known speaker make generalizations about human problems to a mass group of people in an auditorium may have blinded Christians to the fact that they have within the walls of their own church buildings the potentially ideal way of dealing with the individual's questions and hurts.

The Bible is God's own helping program for people, and a caring teacher is the instrument through which it can become more effective than any self-help formula. Note, for example, Psalm 119, in which the Psalmist poetically declares that, in a multitude of specific situations of crisis need, help comes from the Word.

It has been suggested that the use of Scripture is the best way for Christians to do their job of mutual encouragement. The apostle Paul declares that the Word "was written to teach us, so that through endurance and the encouragement of the Scriptures we might have hope" (Romans 15:4).

Actually, the Sunday school has been sold short, for it has always offered much of what people are seeking when they go to counselors. Counseling is a specific type of teaching and learning. Some people need professional counseling, but all need to learn what is taught in Sunday school.

Learning is defined as a change that is the result of conditions other than maturation. That is, if a condition does not develop naturally as a part of the person's physical growth, then it must be learned. This means that since most problems, fears, and excessive emotional discomforts are not the results of instincts, they must be the results of learning of some kind. *Life crises do not inevitably result in overwhelming pain and incapacities.* These responses to problems and crises result because people have not learned how to interpret, and appropriately cope with, their conditions and feelings.

Three important principles emerge from learning theories. First, people learn from past teachings, personal experiences, and examples of others. Individuals can be helped to change if they are given new materials, new experiences, and are motivated to accept alternatives of behavior. Second, the teacher is a vital influence, since he must structure the experiences and motivations so that his students will respond positively. Third, if learning can be appropriated to individual needs, fewer problems can be expected to develop.

Now we come to an idea of tremendous significance to the Christian teacher. Healing of human hurts through learning cannot be completely effective unless people have some assurance that life has real purpose! This assurance comes much more easily to the Christian than to the non-Christian, because the Bible teaches that all experiences have meaning for the believer. "We know that in all things God works for the good of those who love him, who have been called according to His purpose" (Romans 8:28). This truth is not an escape from reality, but a principle of faith that gives a believer stability in times of distress.

The most trusted experts in psychology and counseling say an important connection exists between learning and emotional development. The Bible says it best: "Faith comes from hearing the message, and the message is heard through the word of Christ" (Romans 10:17). If people believe life has meaning and purpose, then life's inevitable discomforts and crises will be seen as meaningful in some way. For example, some of them will be seen as helpful, as experiences that lead to growth and strength for the future.

In his discussion of various counseling theories, Lester Downing considers the concept that one must find meaning and purpose in life—even to the extent of believing that suffering has a purpose—if he is to function effectively and experience happiness.[3] Evidently, Downing is unaware that this concept of suffering having purpose is taught to children in Sunday school; he speaks of this idea as if it were new, calling it "exciting."

To help people find this meaning, Downing suggests *involvement with others* and *manipulation of ideas, translated into action.* He further believes that finding purpose in life will give a person a foundation for building strength to cope with life. All this is done in a good Sunday school.

The foregoing is an example of how persons ignorant of the Word of God try to solve problems that are clearly treated in the Bible, the "textbook" of the Sunday school.

Downing's assertion that people could learn how to cope with problems if they had confidence in the meaning of their lives is a powerful statement. It clearly points out the need for teaching basic Biblical truths. The sure and complete way of dealing with the inevitable is found only in the Word of God. The only absolute assurance of the meaning of life comes through the Word of God, anointed by the Holy Spirit.

RECEPTIVITY TO SPIRITUAL TRUTH DURING CRISES

What is the main theme of most gospel songs and testimonies? Is it not of a brokenness made whole in the Lord? an emptiness filled? a thirsting quenched? How often do you hear of someone in a position of great personal triumph, joy, and success turning to Christ for salvation? Is it not most often from positions of sorrow and weakness that people move toward God?

Secular students often refer to religion as a response to problems that involve uncertainty and powerlessness. The very nature of religion is the acknowledgment of man's inability to meet his ultimate needs. Events in nature, such as famines and tornadoes, are said to underscore man's weakness and inability to control that which greatly affects his well-being. Personal and social happenings as well can have such overwhelming and traumatic qualities that they drive people to look for a transcendent power. The German religious scholar Rudolf Otto says that people are drawn to the *mysterium tremendum*—a power that lies beyond the aspects of reality experienced by human beings—to fill the void in their lives and give meaning to the unknown.[4] Catastrophe, misfortune, and uncontrollable changes plague people, but religion can refer their confusion and distress to a transcendent realm of existence, in terms of which it all makes sense. Human yearning, thirsting, reaching, needing, is proof that we are incomplete and lost without God.

The teacher that understands the relationship between Christian education and human crisis cannot regard the latter merely as an occasion for the demonstration of compassion and love. Instead, he must see it as an opportunity to be used, responsibly and tenderly, to press the claims of Christ. Persons in need require more than caring and sympathy. They require a teacher who will guide them into truth, remembering the words of the Psalmist: "Before I was afflicted I went astray, but now I obey your word. . . . It was good for me to be afflicted so that I might learn your decrees" (Psalm 119:67,71).

GROUPING PROVIDES FAVORABLE LEARNING SITUATIONS

For an individual who has problems and unmet emotional needs, group activity directed toward the goal of a lesson may provide new perspectives from which to view his feelings and attitudes. When the Word is the focus of attention, conditions are right for the Holy Spirit to work, bringing about the appropriate interpretations and applications. Furthermore, many studies have demonstrated that when a person belongs to a supportive group, whatever is learned or experienced is reinforced by the group.

Most people are aware of several kinds of healing and helping groups, such as Weight Watchers and Alcoholics Anonymous. Over two hundred such organizations operate in the United States. It is believed that one of the earliest of these "new group therapies" was a group of tubercular patients, organized in 1907 by Joseph Pratt, a Boston physician.

The history of group work is interesting and significant for our understanding of the role of Bible classes in helping people. We know that group methods were used by Jesus and the Early Church. Most Christians are fond of quoting the words, "Where two or three come together in my name, there am I with them" (Matthew 18:20). We speak of the small group prayer meetings and praise services in houses, as the Early Church took form, and often we long for that kind of intimacy among Christians.

According to Morton Lieberman, who has made thorough studies of the history of group therapies, small groups have served as important healing agents since the beginning of recorded history. He says that group forces have been the instrument for inspiring hope, giving support, and counteracting many emotional and bodily ills. "Religious healers have always relied heavily on group forces, but when healing passed from the priestly to the medical profession, the deliberate use of group forces fell into a decline concomitant with the increasing sanctity of the doctor-patient relationship."[5]

Few Americans realize that the medical profession as we know it is very young. Still in its struggle to become a true science, it has sought to distinguish itself from nonscientific practices. Psychiatrists have been especially anxious to avoid folk practices, and to concentrate on the very private one-to-one aspect of helping people to change or adjust to the crises of life.

But as the helping professions became more established, and experiments such as that of Joseph Pratt came to light, it was acknowledged that most of an individual's ills and problems are related to social factors. Recently great interest has been shown in group methods of helping people through all sorts of problems and physical and emotional needs. It has come to be almost universally accepted by social workers that *helping people means that they are helped to make changes in values and attitudes.* The possibility of bringing about such changes is greatly strengthened through group participation and cohesion.

If a counselor who favors group work is asked to explain why this approach is so effective in bringing about desired results, he may give an answer similar to this: "To the individual, the group can come to represent the total world of social relationships. A person who feels hurt, rejected, victimized, misunderstood, or unworthy is reacting to the way he perceives himself, his world, and the people who have affected his life. In a properly supervised small group, this person begins to realize that he is not so different from others, he is not rejected, he is not unworthy. He can then unlearn some of the fears and behaviors of the past, and develop new ways of feeling, acting, and relating to others."

People have problems, face crises, and suffer trauma and depression not only as individuals but also as part of some social situation and environment. Most people will find adjustment and healing more quickly and completely accomplished if they can feel that they belong and that they are worthy members in the midst of companions. They need opportunities to learn that both independence and dependence are acceptable and possible, and that they can respond to various situations in realistic ways. They need opportunities to contribute, to work in cooperation with others, and to be comfortable in making decisions. All this can be achieved better in group activity than in one-to-one conversations.

Of course the language of the counselor might be much more

technical than what we have used here, but the concepts are accurate.

Just imagine what this means to the teacher of a Bible class! Acting and speaking in Christian love and accepting each person as one for whom Christ died, the proficient teacher can open a whole new world, and structure a new value system. And the teacher does not rely upon the group forces in the same manner as the non-Christian counselor. Christian teachers can rely upon the Heavenly Forces to activate their contributions of good teaching methods and sound Bible content.

Group processes and results such as we have considered might happen in the ideal Sunday school without the teacher being aware of the principles involved, just as good music might be produced by an untrained person who plays by ear. However, the teaching gift, like the music gift, can be made even more effective with knowledge and effort. Therefore it is extremely important that Christian teachers gain the relevant knowledge and develop proficiency in the use of group forces and processes. Here we will examine briefly some of the basic principles, and in the following chapter we will continue with some classroom applications.

Group Dynamics

Most teachers and leaders are somewhat acquainted with the term *group dynamics.* Some people have a tendency to believe that the term refers to exercising enthusiasm and keeping the members of the group active and interested. Actually dynamics is concerned with the interaction of the forces that turn a number of persons into a true group. A Sunday school class can operate rather effectively as a number of individuals if each one is interested in gaining Bible knowledge and the teacher is a skilled and knowledgeable lecturer. Most large sanctuary Bible classes fit this description. They have a place of usefulness in many local church organizations. But if a class is to carry out the function for which it is so potentially capable—the function of *helping to meet the needs of persons*—then it must be a true group.

The noted social psychologist Kurt Lewin set forth the theory that an assembly of persons exists in a "psychological field." This field consists of a number of forces that affect the behavior of the individuals so that they can function together in ways that cannot be explained by individual behavior alone.[6]

Force #1. The capacity of the group to provide a context for comparison. A group can function to help individuals gain insights they might never develop otherwise. For example, each person brings to the assembly a set of experiences. Let's say that John is angry and frustrated because of some experiences. Then, in the group discussion he begins to perceive that Harold has had similar experiences, but he has interpreted them in a different way, and is not frustrated and angry.

As the various members begin to share experiences and their interpretations, a completely new interpretation may emerge, different from that originally held by any one member. It is obvious that this function alone makes group activity in the context of scriptural teaching and Christian testimony a tremendous power for helping anyone who is confused, distressed, or unduly rebellious. Without preaching, scolding, or any manipulating, the teacher who is caring, skilled, and in tune with the guidance of the Holy Spirit can facilitate the operation of this powerful group force.

Force #2. The capacity of the group to develop cohesiveness. A class can experience what Christians sometimes call community. Being in the group becomes very attractive to the individual, and the special warm relationship that develops makes trust and complete acceptance possible among members. In this setting, people tend to feel that they are liked, their self-esteem is lifted, and they may be encouraged to risk revealing needs and requesting prayer. Another positive outcome of cohesiveness is that individuals tend to be loyal and faithful in attendance. This means more teaching and learning opportunities, which increase the chance of working out problems.

Force #3. The capacity of the group to impose social standards. In spite of the prevalent idea that people want to "do their own thing," there seems to be, for most human beings, no reward as sweet as belonging and being accepted as a worthy participant in relationship with others. And there is no punishment as fearsome as being rejected and abandoned. Christians know this, of course, from the spiritual perspective. Acceptance into the family of God is the best reward of heaven, and rejection from His presence is the worst part of hell.

In the group the salutary aspect of social control is that behavior is induced to conform to an acceptable norm. Individuals want to meet the group standards. They do not wish to violate group expectations. And because they are members of a true group (not an assembly of persons being coerced by an authoritarian leader), they feel that they have shared in the formulation of the norms. Most people like to cooperate and conform in a group that helps meet their needs. Therefore, through the group the teacher can most effectively influence the lives of students.

A group has the power to control not only the behavior of its members but their emotions and eventually their attitudes as well. Almost everyone has experienced the stimulation of emotions in a group. Social psychologists have made many studies of crowd and mob behavior, bringing out the negative results of people being carried away and behaving in ways not characteristic of them when they are alone. On the other hand, this group potential to affect emotions can be seen in the positive outcomes of corporate worship, evangelistic services, and the urge to express care and love when the suggestion is made in a Christian context. Unwholesome emotions of self-pity, anger, anxiety, and rebellion can be reduced or eliminated and replaced by feelings of hope, forgiveness, peace, and repentance.

Force #4. The capacity of the group to define reality for its members. One of the main functions of counseling is to bring about insights and self-understanding. People in problem situations often distort reality. Helping them involves leading them to define their condition or situation in realistic terms. As a member of a group, a person gains the perspective of the group on how he should view himself and his condition. Again we can see the relevance of this force when the group is Christian, defining reality from a scriptural point of view. "Do not conform any longer to the pattern of this world, but be transformed by the renewing of your mind. Then you will be able to test and approve what God's will is—his good, pleasing and perfect will" (Romans 12:2).

Sometimes Christians hesitate to admit the importance of group forces, because the idea sounds "humanistic" to them, and they wish to establish their spirituality. The leader of a worship service may say, "Now forget about everyone around you and keep your mind on the Lord." This kind of near-apology for the influence of the group is not necessary. The Bible encourages God's people to assemble for good reasons. Something happens when the group worships together, making the whole idea of religious gatherings meaningful. Otherwise, each person by himself could seek or worship God as well at home. Christian experience has taught us that we need something more, and we cannot avoid the truth that group processes have unique value.

Summary

Sunday school teachers need to recognize the place of their ministry in meeting the needs of individuals who face problems or crisis conditions. Although they are not professional counselors, they minister to people who have problems, and are in a position to be extremely effective helpers. This is true, first, because the Sunday school textbook is the Bible, which contains answers to all human problems. In addition, Christian education programs, such as the Sunday school, operate on many of the same principles as modern Christian counseling. Two of these principles are *learning theory* and *group dynamics.* In the ideal Sunday school class—where people meet in groups to learn from the Word of God under the guidance of a caring and proficient teacher—we find some of the most favorable conditions for meeting human needs.

NOTES

[1]Lawrence J. Crabb Jr., *Effective Biblical Counseling: A Model for Helping Caring Christians Become Capable Counselors* (Grand Rapids, MI: Zondervan, 1977).

[2]Gary R. Collins, *Psychology and Theology* (Nashville, TN: Abingdon, 1981).

[3]Lester N. Downing, *Counseling Theories and Techniques: Summarized and Critiqued* (Chicago: Nelson-Hall, 1975).

[4]Thomas F. O'Dea and Janet O. Avid, *The Sociology of Religion* (Englewood Cliffs, NJ: Prentice-Hall, 1983).

[5]Morton A. Lieberman, *Helping People Change* (Elmsford, NY: Pergamon Press, Inc., 1980), p. 472.

[6]Kurt Lewin, "Group Decision and Social Change," *Readings in Social Philosophy,* Newcomb and Hartley eds. (New York: Henry Holt, 1974).

2

The Teacher Is Part of Every Lesson

The attitudes and behavior of teachers determine the effectiveness of the Sunday school.

Research tells us that our brains do not operate in simple stimulus-response terms, nor do they simply store facts for future reference. Instead, our brains are magnificent organs for the discovery and creation of meaning. Our brains constantly seek to make sense of inner and outer experience. We are seekers and creators of meaning and the meanings we create determine the ways we behave.[1]

These words were written by a noted educator, Arthur W. Combs, in an article explaining the importance of what is called affective education. The term *affective* is used to distinguish the emotional processes surrounding learning from the mere intellectual processes. Combs believes that learning is essentially a process of discovering personal meaning, and that a teacher, even of the basic school subjects, who ignores the importance of feelings, emotions, and attitudes may fail to bring about learning. According to Combs, four factors critically influence the learning process: (1) self-concept, (2) feelings of challenge or threat, (3) the value system, and (4) feelings of belonging and being cared for.

If this is true in the teaching of the conventional school subjects, think how much more the concept may apply to Sunday school teaching. Not only is it possible for the Christian teacher to minister to personal and emotional conditions of the students, without such personal ministry it is impossible to teach the Bible with maximum effectiveness.

Clearly from the example of Jesus, the teacher is an important part of every learning situation. Jesus' presentation of materials and principles to be learned always included a personal relationship with those who received His teaching. In today's textbooks on social work methods, the "use of self" is listed as a *skill* to be developed and used in helping clients. The relationship between the client and the helper must be established before any method or treatment can become effective. Walter Friedlander suggests three main elements must be present in all successful social work.[2]

1. The counselor and the client must develop a personal relationship.

2. The counselor must make accurate observations in order to determine the needs of the client.

3. The counselor must make suitable application of the resources at the client's disposal to help him gain insights into his own needs and find ways of solving his own problems.

In the Christian education setting, the same three elements are needed. Teachers must be true Christian friends, in positions of respect but approachable and warm. They must be sensitive to the needs of the students, aware of problems and crisis situations. The resources, the Scriptures, and the classroom situation must be used to meet the needs of the students. The students must be helped to appropriate truth and make personal applications, receiving for themselves the healing power available in Christ.

To accomplish these ends, teachers need to develop three characteristics: (1) empathy, (2) sense of mission, and (3) proficiency.

Empathy

Empathy means the condition of putting oneself into the thoughts and feelings of another and perceiving the world as he does. It is a combination of understanding (in the sense of knowing with the mind how another feels) and then feeling along with him. Counselors and social workers in training are required to do roleplaying exercises in which they try to become as much as possible like the expected client. They ride in wheelchairs, walk with crutches, wear blindfolds, and spend time in jails and hospitals.

Certainly Christian teachers should be as concerned as counselors with the development of empathy. They can imagine how they might feel if they were terminally ill, abandoned by a loved one, or in the position of an adolescent. Prayerfully and thoughtfully teachers can study each Sunday school lesson, seeking an appropriate application for each condition a student in the class might represent. In the following chapters a number of specific crisis situations are described. The teacher must understand the conditions so that misconceptions and lack of information will not stand in the way of his empathy.

Sense of Mission

Teachers are called of God and gifted by His Spirit to carry out their ministry. That is, the "gifting" is to provide the essential functions of teaching in the church. When teachers become aware of this privilege and responsibility of fulfilling a unique part of God's plan, of being His co-workers—this awareness we call a *sense of mission.* Sunday school teachers impart information and stimulate the development of attitudes and behaviors that will result in mature, productive Christians. Counselors and social workers see their main goal as helping people *change* their values and their conceptions of themselves and others. The central goal of all Christian teaching is to *establish* God's values and give real meaning to life, from childhood to old age.

In regard to human crises and problems, the central mission of the teacher is to keep the world's values and behavioral patterns from seriously affecting Christians and all those who seek refuge in the Word of God, to help people build lives that cannot be torn apart by disappointments, bereavement, pain, human weakness, traumatic experiences, and the inevitable changes of life.

There is a saying that "children brought up in Sunday school are seldom brought up in court." This is true in principle. Those who develop Christian values from childhood, and are given opportunities for consistent teaching and associations with practicing, caring Christians, are seldom overwhelmed by the events of life. The most important determinant in a human life is the teaching and influence received in the home. If the home is Christian, then the Sunday school teacher is its best ally, reinforcing the home experience. If the home is not Christian, then the Sunday school may be a child's only hope for building a foundation of values and attitudes that will provide the strength to face life's inevitable changes and unexpected calamities.

No Christian worker ever received a higher calling or a more challenging assignment than this. Yet there is more to the Sunday school teacher's task. In addition to the primary ministry of prevention, he must help meet the needs of those whose strengths have not been developed previously. Those who need immediate relief will be in the class, as well as those who have doubts, questions, fears, temptations, and rebellious spirits.

Included also in the teacher's mission, or specialized function in the church community, is that of being a support service for the pastor and professionals who may be working with members of the class. A person who is receiving counseling usually is in need of much personal attention and concern. The knowledge and assurance of warmth and love, that someone is interested, can make a person's response to counseling more positive. It is obvious, too, that the work of a Christian counselor is facilitated when his client has Biblical knowledge. Surely a caring, competent Bible teacher is a silent partner of all who do pastoral or other professional counseling.

This kind of involvement with individuals and their needs can be exhausting. Teachers become frustrated, disillusioned, and filled with self-doubt when their students seem to fail. Only the sense of mission—the assurance of divine calling and purpose—can keep teachers genuinely interested, eager, loving, and willing to develop their gifts through prayer, study, and training.

Proficiency

The need of preparing for the mental activities of Sunday school, for the impartation of knowledge, is obvious. Not so obvious is the need for preparing for ministry to those human needs that go beyond a lack of information to matters of the heart, to the emotional nature of man. The Sunday school teacher should be proficient in both areas.

It is almost impossible to overemphasize the knowledge, experience, and skill—*proficiency*—needed in Sunday school teaching. The proficient teacher has credibility. Students are likely to accept his word and act upon his suggestions. The proficient teacher maintains attention and interest, and creates a tone of authenticity in the classroom. The proficient teacher is comfortable and free, unthreatened by questions and comments from the class. The proficient teacher gives appropriate answers to questions involving Biblical facts and doctrines so that students not only gain knowledge but are influenced to receive God's Word and make personal applications.

Most human problems involve feelings of doubt, insecurity, uncertainty, indecision, and questions concerning meaning and purpose. The proficient teacher provides stability, reason, wisdom, and confidence. Furthermore, the teacher who is well prepared and not worried about his own activities is able to give attention to the individuals in the class. Needs and troubles can be discerned and given appropriate consideration. Teachers who are unsure of their own abilities tend to feel impatient at intrusions or distractions; whereas competent teachers may welcome these as indications from the Lord to guide the class in a certain direction.

Thus we see that the proficiencies usually expected of teachers, such as knowledge of the Bible, Christian doctrine, and instructional principles, are closely related to providing emotional supports. In addition to these general proficiencies, we must consider some more specific types of knowledge and skills required for maximum success in ministering to critical human needs.

UNDERSTANDING INDIVIDUALS AS WHOLE PERSONS

In the conventional Sunday school training activity, teachers are divided into groups according to the ages or classes they teach. Much attention is given to the general characteristics to be expected at each stage of human development. This is an essential aspect of teacher education. Often overlooked, however, is the fact that *every* person passes through the various stages. Ryan, who is now a primary, will become a teenager and a senior citizen. Virginia, who is now a senior citizen, was once a primary and a teenager. Since everyone will normally pass through each of the stages, the teacher is constantly receiving the product of other teachers and preparing the product for other teachers. Every stage is critical for developing people who will confront life's inevitable crises and suffer its unexpected calamities. Therefore, all teachers are responsible for understanding not only the characteristics of their own students, but something of the other stages of human growth and development. As we shall see, for example, when we consider unmarried mothers, most of the factors leading to their condition are related to previous failures at learning and understanding.

A teacher who understands the needs of children is better equipped to deal with the problems of parents. One who understands the critical needs of parents is more competent to guide the behavior of adolescents. One familiar with the realities of mid-life crisis is better qualified to minister to an elderly parent who feels neglected by a middle-aged son.

Sunday school training activities should provide opportunities for teachers to share information and discuss the characteristics, needs, and problems of their various groups. If the leadership does not provide this, individual teachers should assume the responsibility of sharing with one another.

UNDERSTANDING INDIVIDUALS AS SETS OF ROLES AND RELATIONSHIPS

Almost every human problem and condition involves roles and relationships. As an individual, everyone is a son or daughter. But think how many other relationships are possible: brother or sister, spouse, parent, grandchild, grandparent, cousin, uncle or aunt, niece or nephew, ex-spouse, stepchild, stepparent, student, teacher, employee, employer, member, official, citizen, neighbor—and many more.

Associated with each relationship is a set of expected behavior patterns, obligations, and privileges. For example, within a mother-daughter relationship, the mother is expected to act one way and her daughter another. But if the daughter is also a mother, she is expected to act in another way within her second relationship. These sets of expected behaviors are called roles. It is easy to see in this simple illustration that you cannot know exactly what to expect of a person unless you know what role he is in at the time.

With many relationships and complex sets of expectations, it is no wonder that people become confused. (We will consider this more fully in the chapter on identity crisis.) Without some knowledge of what roles are required of their students and what problems arise as a result of conflicts and misunderstanding between the student and those to whom he relates in his various roles, teachers cannot understand their students' needs.

AWARENESS OF CONDITIONS AND GENERAL ATTITUDES WITHIN THE COMMUNITY

Teachers can minister more effectively if they are aware of conditions, values, and attitudes that prevail in their community. Television programs, happenings in the local schools, articles in popular magazines—these are the kinds of influences that affect the attitudes and behaviors of those who attend our Sunday schools. Notions such as self-assertiveness, personal fulfillment, rights, self-love; tolerance of questionable practices related to sex, use of drugs, types of entertainment—

these are some features of changing value systems that lead to dissatisfaction and unrest. Lawrence Crabb, author of *Effective Biblical Counseling,* believes that many of the problems people have are related to *problem thinking,* in regard to these types of values. Many people, for example, believe that fulfillment means having their selfish desires gratified. Crabb says they must redefine their concepts in the light of Christian truth before they can find true happiness and emotional health.[3]

Sunday school teachers can be powerful forces in the shaping of emotionally healthy Christians—but only by staying abreast of changing social values that affect their students. Teachers should read local newspapers and current periodicals, especially the news magazines, and watch informative TV documentaries on issues such as sexual practices, alcohol and drug abuse, divorce, unemployment, and aging. Class members should be given opportunities to mention some of their reading and viewing experiences so the teacher will know what sorts of influences are at work in their lives. High school and college students might be invited to bring some of their textbooks to class to illustrate current teachings on sex, marriage practices, death and dying, and other relevant social concerns. Newspaper clippings can be brought as illustrations of personal and social concerns. A class activity might involve the consideration of these in the light of Christian values and Biblical truth.

The teacher must be well informed, and he must handle such materials as an educator. That is, the expression of shock or condemnation directed against people or institutions has no place in the classroom. When facts are presented as they exist in the real world, and the Biblical truth is allowed to speak for itself, then the Sunday school is contributing as it should to meet the current needs and conditions of the students.

FAMILIARITY WITH THE CHURCH PROGRAM AND LOCAL RESOURCES

This may seem too obvious to mention, but each Sunday school teacher is obligated to be acquainted with all the services and opportunities in the local church. The teacher should keep informed about openings for service to which students might be referred, and activities that might be helpful to the members of students' families. Seminars, retreats, discussion groups, Bible studies, special interest events, field trips—these can be important experiences for people who feel lonely, rejected, depressed, or want to make Christian contacts or to be of service. The office hours and phone number of people able to help should be close to the teacher's telephone so that callers can be given specific information.

The community may have helping facilities for people experiencing needs or emergencies, for example, child abuse. The teacher should be informed about such community services, able to refer people to the most appropriate facilities. For example, a crisis center may be sponsored by a Christian group. If the opportunity exists, the teacher should become acquainted with Christian counselors, and their services, to whom referrals may be made.

As a general rule, if serious problems arise or are anticipated, the teacher should inform the pastor of the situation and request his advice before making referrals to professionals or to community facilities.

GENERAL UNDERSTANDING OF HUMAN EMOTIONAL NEEDS

Persons of various ages have similar feelings and emotional needs. We might call these the general needs. (They come in specific packages relative to each age and condition.)

1. The need to relate to someone and be accepted, to be loved and to love
2. The need to accept the self, justify self to self
3. The need for meaning, the security of knowing how one is to relate and what to expect, predictability, order
4. The need for some kind of success feeling, achievement

In each of the following chapters we will consider which of these needs is involved in a given kind of crisis, and what combination of unmet needs results in emotional problems, discomfort, or inability to cope. This will make it possible for the teacher to understand better the behavior of the students, and to utilize most effectively the tools available in the Sunday school setting.

For example, a child's need to be accepted might lead to unruly behavior in class; whereas a teenager with the same need might use drugs, or even decide to have a baby. The teacher who understands that people of all ages have the same general needs will not use the Bible lessons only as a way of proving a given behavior is wrong. Instead, the scriptural lessons can be applied so that needs are met in Christian ways, and the incorrect ways are shown to be destructive to the person as well as sinful in the sight of God. Thus the behavior can be modified by genuine change in the person—and that is the true purpose of Christian education.

Understanding human needs can lead to more effective use of Bible teaching in yet another way. Teachers will realize that emotional needs are not exactly the same as spiritual needs. This is not to say that sin is not the root of all problems, or that spiritual healing will not bring about healing for the entire person. Sin is the basic cause of all suffering, and Christ is the only ultimate cure. Nevertheless, Christians suffer, and sometimes break emotionally in times of personal crises.

Our evangelical background has given most of us the impression that spiritual healing comes instantaneously. We believe that a person who has partaken of every sin and knows nothing of God can walk into an evangelistic service, feel conviction, repent, confess his sins, be saved, and walk out a born-again Christian. Therefore, we have a tendency to be impatient with persons who have emotional problems. We want to say, "Just lean on Jesus, trust Him with all your cares, and everything will be all right."

Psychologists, on the other hand, speak of working through problems. They believe that most healing is in stages, and in some cases it is necessary to pass through one stage in order to arrive at another. One of the most widely known series of stages is Dr. Kubler-Ross' stages of dying. In personal interviews with terminally ill patients and studies of their behaviors, Dr. Kubler-Ross isolated stages through which most individuals pass from the time they learn that they are terminally ill until the time of their death. These stages are shock, denial, anger, depression, bargaining, and, finally, acceptance.[4]

Scholars in the various behavioral sciences have recognized that responses in other types of crises resemble the Kubler-Ross stages of dying. It has been found that grief and the experiences following divorce can be explained in similar terms. The national Sunday School Department of the Assemblies of God formulated what they call the Crisis Time Line.[5] Assuming that a crisis is a point at which a particular life-style is traumatically ended (as in the death of a spouse or a divorce), or is recognized as inappropriate or destructive (as in substance abuse), the Crisis Time Line proposes the following stages: *Life-style,* crisis, denial, anger, bargaining, depression. These are the downward steps of reactions to the situation. Then come the steps to recovery: acceptance, forgiveness, faith, confidence, growth, and then *new life-style.*

This conceptualization of emotional stages can be very useful to the teacher for understanding the needs of students in a class, even without an attempt at one-to-one helping in the professional sense. The teacher should not expect immediate response to persuasive messages. Don't try to convince a student that his problem is easily solved, or that his feelings are not valid. The Bible teaching situation provides almost unlimited opportunity to help a person work through grief, problems, and personal weaknesses by giving scriptural examples and guidance in comprehension of God's love and provision. Surely the teacher, as well as the Bible characters in the lessons, serves as a model for the *new life-style,* and Christian class members provide mutual support. Indeed the Sunday school class can be an ideal environment for this process of growth out of crisis and into a new way of life!

Summary

In this chapter we have emphasized that the attitudes and behaviors of teachers determine the effectiveness of the teaching. Ministering to the personal and emotional needs of students is necessary for maximum educational results. We proposed that effective teachers retain a trio of characteristics: *empathy, sense of mission,* and *proficiency.*

Four major proficiencies were treated: (1) The teacher must understand students as whole persons, rather than as age-groupings. (2) The teacher must understand the significance of roles and relationships in the development of individual personalities. (3) The teacher must be familiar with all resources in the church and the community that might be useful in helping students. (4) The teacher must understand the nature of emotional needs and the responses that people make in times of crises and problem situations.

NOTES

[1] Arthur W. Combs, "Affective Education or None at All," *Educational Leadership,* April 1982, pp. 495-497.

[2] Walter A. Friedlander, ed. *Concepts and Methods of Social Work* (Englewood Cliffs, NJ: Prentice-Hall, 1976).

[3] Lawrence J. Crabb, Jr., *Effective Biblical Counseling: A Model for Helping Caring Christians Become Capable Counselors* (Grand Rapids, MI: Zondervan, 1977).

[4] Elisabeth Kubler-Ross, *On Death and Dying* (New York: MacMillan Publishing Co., Inc., 1969).

[5] *Sunday School Counselor,* April 1983, pp. 6-8.

3

Single Parents and Blended Families

Good teachers accept the students as they are today; then work and pray for a different tomorrow.

The idea that people marry for keeps and struggle through for the sake of the children is gone. The children of the ME GENERATION are in terrible trouble.

The rise of suicides among adolescents, drug abuse, teenage pregnancies, alcoholism, and crime prove the point.[1]

These are not the words of a conservative evangelist. They were spoken at a meeting of the American Academy of Pediatrics, by Dr. Derek Miller, head of the adolescent unit at Northwestern Memorial Hospital in Chicago.

Statistics on marriage and the family are overwhelming. In these times of rapid change, accuracy is impossible, but it can be said with confidence that about 40 percent of the first time marriages in the United States end in divorce. Over 80 percent of the affected parties remarry within 3 years, and over 40 percent of the second marriages also end in divorce. Studies concerning unmarried mothers reveal that 40 percent of girls in the United States between the ages of 15 and 19 are sexually active. In this age-group there are over a million pregnancies each year. Thirty thousand pregnancies are recorded annually among girls of 13 and 14 years of age. The average age of the pregnant teenager is 14.5 years. Of the women heading families, 11 percent have never been married.[2]

According to 1980 census figures, 19 percent of the families with children were single parent families. Of these, 90 percent were maintained by mothers and 10 percent by fathers. About half the nearly 12 million children involved were children of divorce. Over 1.5 million were children of unmarried teenagers.

The following comparison indicates that the incidence of single parent households has increased considerably.

Families headed by females
1970—5,591,000
1979—8,458,000
Children living with mother only
1970—7,501,000
1979—10,543,000
Children living with father only
1970—764,038
1979—998,224

Nearly half the children in school live in households with single parents. Then, of course, with the high rate of remarriage comes an increasing formation of stepfamilies, or blended families. If the current trend continues, the blended families will soon outnumber the exclusively biological families.

In response to this situation, textbook writers and social service agencies are searching for new definitions for the term *family*. The critical nature of the situation is thus illustrated by the fact that no one seems to know exactly what a family is!

Most sociologists believe that because the family has the essential functions of providing for physical and emotional needs, it will continue to exist in some form. As one scholar has expressed it: "The family is amazingly persistent as a social institution. What is changing is the definition. . . . The nuclear family pattern is being replaced by the notion of the impermanence of marriage. . . . Thus the pattern of marriage—divorce—remarriage is likely to hold, so long as large numbers of American women remain in the labor force and laws continue to make divorce a realistic option."[3]

The reaction of some Christian leaders to words such as these is to denounce the textbooks. They say the textbooks are giving young persons a wrong idea of marriage, leading to the destruction of the family.

A more sensible reaction would be to analyze the realities of the situation. Most textbook writers feel obliged to speak in terms of what is, not what ought to be. In many cases they are making sincere efforts to help students understand what is happening to their world. Unfortunately, this matter-of-fact acceptance of prevailing conditions leaves little room for children and parents to understand the dangers and evils involved.

Not only Christian leaders, but many professionals in the fields of psychiatry and mental health believe that easy divorce is the wrong solution to family problems, and that keeping the marriage together for the sake of the children is better than destroying the children by divorce. And, while the secular books merely describe what is, the Sunday school teachers are in a uniquely significant position to speak out for what ought to be on the basis of Scripture, and, even more important, what *can be* on the basis of Christian love.

In some cases divorce may be justifiable; the teacher is not required to offer personal judgment. To admit a condition exists is neither to judge nor support it. To accept those who are affected by a condition is not to approve or to condemn their behavior. The simple truth is that if the Sunday school is reaching out as it should be, then half those in attendance may come from homes that are different from the idealized model. To overlook this and ignore the resultant special needs of people would be unrealistic and unpardonably neglectful.

To effectively focus the teaching ministry, the teacher must know how the changing conditions of family life and structure are likely to affect the students. One case may differ greatly from another. Some individuals handle life situations with little trauma, and others are devastated. Because of this, making general assumptions is unwise.

In the following pages we will consider several types of families, probably represented in every Sunday school. These will include families headed by single parents (as a result of death, divorce, or unmarried motherhood) and families blended by remarriage. Teachers of children, teachers of young people, teachers of adults—all become involved with members of such families. Their responsibility is to be prepared for ministry to any of these within the context of the teaching position. Basic to this preparation is awareness of the needs and problems most characteristic of these persons.

Understanding the Conditions

Single parents and stepparents share a similar crisis, that is, a transition experience that disrupts and changes their way of life. This means that the manner in which their basic needs were being met is no longer available. One who experienced this transition said, "We are a whole new species of the human person. It's like waking up in a totally different world."

Adjustments must be made physically and emotionally to survive a crisis. Most problems and needs cluster within the following areas:

1. Emotional
2. Sexual
3. Social
4. Kinship relations
5. Financial

The caring and competent teacher will keep these areas of need in mind while preparing a lesson, and will seek the Holy Spirit's guidance in making the appropriate applications from Scripture.

PERSONAL EMOTIONS

Becoming single after being married is emotionally exhausting. Both the death of, and a divorce from, a spouse is described by psychologists as "loss" that results in emotional anguish, and sometimes prolonged stress symptoms. Death often is preceded by the stress of seeing a loved one suffer, and divorce may be preceded by the turmoil of a bitter legal battle. No person comes through either of these events without emotional trauma and shock. Most people experience a sequence of emotions similar to those described in the Dr. Kubler-Ross model (see chapter 2, p. 31).

Some debilitating emotions that may accompany divorce are guilt, shame, self-doubt, feelings of rejection, anger, self-pity, desire for revenge, and feelings of failure. In addition to causing bereavement, the death of a spouse may bring about acute remorse, regrets, guilt, and self-accusation. Becoming a single parent, by whatever means, usually results in feelings of helplessness, indecision, isolation, and anxiety about the needs of the children and plans for the future.

Unmarried mothers usually are subject to even greater emotional stress than other single parents. They may feel guilty, and, at the same time, angry with, and rebellious against, society. As difficult as it may be for some adults to understand this, studies reveal that many young girls fail to connect sexual activity with the real possibility of pregnancy. It is not that they do not know physical facts, but that they are influenced by what Jules Henry calls "cultural dreams." In the world of advertising the ideas expressed are not intended to be taken literally. For example, we know the claims of toothpaste ads concerning sex appeal are fictitious. Yet that appeal will cause millions of consumers to select that brand.

Similarly, sexual activity is portrayed by the media as a common part of modern social life. Many young people do not think in terms of real life consequences. When girls become pregnant, they may feel resentful and betrayed. Their romantic adventures led them into unexpected problems. Some girls declare they were just unlucky. They often express hostility toward anyone who tries to befriend them. They hesitate to trust anyone.

In some cases, hostility is a cause rather than an effect. Some girls decide to become pregnant as a form of punishment for those who have failed to provide for their needs. Their need to receive and express love may seem to be met by having a baby. Some girls have said they wanted babies because they were lonely, and others said it was to demonstrate their independence.

The stepfamily situation almost certainly engenders significant personal stress. Personality traits of the individuals are intensified. Conditions are conducive to feelings of rejection, jealousy, competition, displacement, anger, guilt, and divided loyalties. Confusion, irritability, and anxiety are present to some degree in almost every blended household.

SEXUAL READJUSTMENT

Virginia Smith in *The Single Parent* writes:

> To say there is no sexual adjustment after an individual becomes single is to hide one's head in the sand. . . . When separation deprives an individual of this important aspect of a marriage relationship, common sense tells us there must be a void.[4]

Advertisers, script writers for television, and editors of modern magazines do not have their heads in the sand. They exploit the situation of the single parent with a constant bombardment of sex talk. Singles are encouraged to be sexually liberated. Some women's magazines, once devoted to home and family, now give explicit advice on sexual activities.

Deprived of the satisfaction of normal desires, and stimulated by the sexual orientation of the society, singles tend to react in extreme ways. They may completely accept the world's values and justify their behavior on the basis of natural instinct. Some may try, consciously or unconsciously, to use sex as an escape from problems, or as proof of their attractiveness and worth.

Some singles take the opposite extreme and try to deny their feelings. They feel guilty and believe that people will judge them on the basis of the media image. Some women fear, perhaps with reason, that they are victims of those who consider singles (especially divorced and unmarried mothers) to be easy marks for sexual aggression. Christian singles who have given in to physical impulses often become convinced that they are hopeless sinners.

Many members of blended families are faced with new and difficult situations involving their sexuality. Confusion may result as step siblings try to relate to one another. Spouses may become suspicious and jealous of their stepchildren. Minor disagreements can become major conflicts when the members of the blended family are trying to establish their positions in the new situation. Even the matter of how to dress in the home can cause stress and undue awareness of sexuality for step siblings.

SOCIAL FACTORS

Few people seem to understand the significance of social role in personality. In American society, and perhaps paradoxically even more so in the church, the emphasis is upon individuality. The doctrine of free will leads to the interpretation of behavior as essentially a result of personal choice and an indication of individual personality traits. The importance of a person's having a safely defined social role with a clear set of behavioral expectations may not become apparent until his life is disrupted. Becoming "suddenly single" causes the individual to realize how much of his behavior was determined by role expectations. Often this new world of choice and responsibility creates what is called identity crises.

Personal identity crisis will be discussed in chapter 10. The emphasis at this point is upon the adjustments that must be made when social relationships are changed in some way. All members of single parent and blended families face these adjustments, and their situations cannot be understood without recognition of this fact.

Nothing can change completely the fact that divorced and widowed persons and unmarried girls who have become mothers are not accepted as the same persons they were before. Society has given them a different identity and has established a different set of expectations. They do not belong in the same way. They do not fit in the same places. They must accept new social roles. We speak not of what ought to be, but of what is, both outside and inside the church community.

Divorced people and unmarried mothers may feel that society

looks upon them as failures. They may have broken the moral code of their society and be exposed to ridicule and condemnation. They may actually lose friends—or imagine they do. If they have been taught as Christians, they may be acutely aware of their unacceptable position. They draw away in guilt from old acquaintances, and are afraid to reveal themselves to new ones. They may feel that they are an embarrassment to their families and friends.

Widowed persons may feel that they are the objects of pity, or that they are being avoided because others do not know how to relate to them as single persons. Relationships once maintained through the husband, such as those with business associates, must now be formed directly by the widow.

Special holidays, birthdays, and occasions with social significance may become extremely painful for those whose roles have changed; such occasions usually have their meaning in family traditions. Those who withdraw at these times from social contacts suffer loneliness, even though their isolation is seen by others as self-imposed.

For unmarried mothers the change in social status usually is dramatic. The majority drop out of school. They are separated from former friends and activities and are at a tremendous disadvantage in the establishment of new relationships. They may be stigmatized by society not only on the basis of morality, but because they add unwanted children to the population and create tax burdens and other problems.

KINSHIP RELATIONS

The most significant social roles are kinship relations. Usually divorce and remarriage do not end relationships, only complicate them. Divorced parents maintain contacts because of visitation rights, child support, and various crises in the lives of the children. Some families make relatively comfortable adjustments, but others experience years of bitter disputes and lasting hurts.

Some believe divorce is better for children than an unhappy

family, but most scholars who have studied the question thoroughly contend that the bad marriage is less injurious to children than is divorce. Separation and divorce is a frightening experience that threatens the self-worth of children. Frequently they feel they are to blame and are being punished. Children try desperately to bring their parents back together. No one can say how great is the long term effect of this experience.

For unmarried mothers, also, kinship relations can be painful. Often they are alienated from parents who feel embarrassed and hurt. The pregnant girl's mother may express feelings of personal injury, such as, "How could you do this to us?" Then, when the baby comes, the young mother may express her frustration by abusing the infant.

The blended household has the potential for every sort of kinship problem. Rather than gradually grown from biological seed, a new family must be structured immediately from ready-made components. Multiple adjustments must be made simultaneously among spouses, children, stepchildren, stepparents, ex-spouses, and relatives, including several sets of grandparents, uncles, and aunts.

Grandparents, as well as ex-spouses, have begun to ask the courts for *their* rights. Children are told to "be nice" on the basis of some obligation they do not understand. Love and acceptance can no longer be taken for granted but somehow has come to be based upon special behaviors and implied rivalries.

To add to the uncertainty, there are no established forms of address to use in all family situations. What do you call people who fill these roles but are not *really* Dad, Mom, Sis, or Grandma?

FINANCES

Most single parents and blended families encounter financial problems. Men may be burdened by alimony and child support payments to one household and be unable to provide adequately for a new family. On the other hand, many fathers fail to comply with child support agreements.

Often, widowed and divorced mothers have little work experience or career preparation. Unmarried mothers who have dropped out of school usually earn meager wages. In order to work, a mother must pay for child care. These conditions cause lower standards of living and create the need for welfare assistance. The custodial parent may move into poor housing, possibly putting the children into neighborhoods where their opportunities or "life chances" are greatly decreased. The parent is burdened with anxiety for the future, and perhaps with guilt as well for not being able to provide better. Overwork and worry will have both emotional and physical consequences for every member of the family.

What Can a Teacher Do?

We have taken the first step toward successful teaching now that we have assumed the viewpoint that the purpose of our work is to meet specific needs of people whom God has entrusted to us. We have recognized the scope of the condition and described some of the characteristics and needs of those who may be in our classes. The next step is to think in practical terms and outline some suggestions to guide our action.

GENERAL SUGGESTIONS

1. Be aware and sensitive so that nothing is said to embarrass individuals whose family situation is different from the ideal model. Avoid using the term "broken home."

2. Accept individuals as they are, without asking reasons for their circumstances, or make personal judgments and evaluations of their behavior.

3. Pray for insight to use the Scriptures effectively without making reference to any individual case.

4. See that treatment of special days and social events is appropriate for everyone and takes into consideration the feelings of all members of the class.

5. Provide activities that give opportunities for lonely persons to become acquainted with Christian peers. Be sure to introduce people to one another. Learn and use the correct names. Seek to develop a true group.

6. Be prepared to make referrals to a pastor or other helping person or agency when you recognize critical needs.

Suggestions for teachers of children

Children of divorce and children who have lost a parent tend to feel guilty, as though they are somehow to blame for the situation. Usually their loss and fear are complicated by confusion. They need most of all to be accepted warmly and naturally, and to be part of a group where pleasant activity is honest and spontaneous.

Be aware of the possibility that a child has two addresses, and may spend his time in two different households. Enrollment forms should provide adequate space to record this information. Invitations to parents and carry-home items must be provided in duplicate for those who have divided households.

Be sensitive in the use of illustrations concerning family activities. Beware of the stereotyped image of stepparents, and the assumption that a father is always a person who is loving and protective.

Be sensitive to the feelings that may be aroused by Christmas, Mother's Day, and Father's Day.

Suggestions for teachers of adolescents

Research indicates that the persons most affected by changes in the family situation may be adolescents. At a time when they are seeking their own identity, they are thrown into confusion. Their loyalties are divided by divorce and remarriage, and their status in the home may be changed radically. They may be drawn into peer group associations that lead to the use of drugs and alcohol, or other questionable activities. The Sunday school class can provide Christian peer group support, and may represent the only real stability the adolescent knows.

Be honest and accepting with adolescents. Do not display shock. Allow them to express themselves without fear of being criticized. Keep their confidences, and do not discuss outside of the classroom what they have revealed of themselves and their concerns.

To be accepting of people is not to refrain from expressing Biblical truth in very clear terms. Do not allow a spirit of argument, but read the Bible and explain what it has to say about the issues in question.

Do not hesitate to inform young people of the dangers and heartaches that result from drugs, alcohol, rebellion against social norms, and sexual activity outside of marriage. Seek the Lord's guidance for confronting these subjects without embarrassment, but with honesty and love.

Suggestions for teachers of older adults

Be aware that older adults are deeply affected by the marriage problems of their offspring. Sometimes their feelings of loss and grief are as great as those of the immediate family, and they should be treated with equal compassion. Sometimes they are deprived of contact with their grandchildren. They feel that they have failed or may be to blame in some way. They are hurt, resentful, and shocked at the change in values that make divorce and remarriage seem casual and acceptable.

Do not allow discussions of these matters to take on tones of self-righteousness or condemnation of the younger generation. Help the older people see how they can provide love and support. Guide them in prayer for the families of the church.

Discuss with the class the organization of a child-care service to assist single parents.

God Trusts Us With People Who Need Us

In Exodus 32, a most remarkable conversation between God and Moses is recorded. The people had made an idol, and God expressed His displeasure. He said to Moses, "Go down, your people have become corrupt." Notice that God said "your" people. God had called Moses and given him the task of leading the people out of bondage. Now He was angry with them. But Moses spoke back to God: "O Lord, why should your anger burn against your people?" Notice that Moses also said, "your" people. They were the people of God and they were the people of Moses. God had made Moses responsible for them during this particular journey. Moses accepted the responsibility. He went back to "own" them, in whatever condition they were, and led them on as God would direct him toward the Promised Land.

The responsibilities of teachers can be compared figuratively with those of Moses. Within a certain context, some people are entrusted to us by the Lord. We accept them, "own" them as our responsibility—in whatever condition they are, whether they arrived there through sin or innocence. The focus of our ministry is upon these people. Every word of Scripture, every line in the lesson manual, every method and technique we have learned, should be interpreted in the light of their needs.

Summary

The single parent and the remarried now comprise a large percentage of the social unit defined as "family." To effectively minister to students of such families, the teacher must understand how these changing conditions of family life and structure affect each member of that family.

Social, emotional, sexual, and financial adjustments as well as adjustments in relationships with relatives must be made to survive a transition in family structure and the way basic needs are met. Teachers must be knowledgeable and sensitive so that nothing is said to embarrass those class members adjusting to new situations. Remember that God has entrusted you with individuals who must be accepted as they are!

NOTES

[1]*The News-Leader,* 3 April 1983, p. 8G.

[2]*Ibid.*

[3]Richard Bourne and Jack Levin, *Social Problems: Causes, Consequences, Interventions* (St. Paul, MN: West Publishing Co., 1983), p. 301.

[4]Virginia Watts Smith, *The Single Parent* (Old Tappan, NJ: Fleming Revell Co., 1982), p. 96.

4

The Trauma of Adolescence

How can a young man keep his way pure? By living according to Your word (Psalm 119:9).

Adolescence was invented in the United States! In 1904, G. Stanley Hall, who was the first president of the American Psychological Association, used this term to describe a period of "storm and stress" between childhood and adulthood. Before this time, descriptions of the life cycle did not include a separate categorical term to designate the years from early teens to early twenties.

Those who know the Bible are well acquainted with the terms childhood and youth, but even these terms are missing in accounts of preindustrial societies. People were considered infants until about the time of puberty, when they were ritually accepted into the society as adults. Although references to problems caused by a generation gap are found in the earliest recorded histories, the specific concerns, which we know as adolescent turmoil, seem to have developed from the rapid social changes of more recent times.

Problems of adolescence are commonly attributed to transition. Yet seldom is this radical change analyzed. Americans tend to think of childhood as opposite of adulthood. Children are to be cared for and protected. Adults are responsible for their own welfare and morally responsible for their own behavior. Children are to obey their parents and teachers. Adults are expected to make the rules and see that children obey them. A person must completely reverse his behavior between the time he is perceived as a child and when he is perceived as an adult. But there is no specified age or accomplishment that establishes the person as an adult. He is expected at one time to make sensible decisions and behave in a responsible manner, and at another time to accept what seem to be childish restrictions, such as arbitrary rules. The ambiguity is not in the individual only, but in the society as well. We have no definite point at which individuals are pronounced adults and given a clear set of expectations.

The definition of crisis as a disruption of a usual state, where needs are no longer met as before and new ways of meeting them must be found, seems to fit this adolescent period. Psychologists and sociologists have used the terms *marginal* and *uncertainty of belongingness* to describe the condition of adolescence. Possibly no other human crisis presents so great an opportunity for help being provided through the educational process. Much of what has been described as rebellion in teenagers may be better understood as a kind of striving to learn, to unlearn, and to relearn. The Sunday school teacher is in a strategic position to help these young people understand the nature of their own needs, and learn how to meet them in ways that will lead to the joys and satisfactions of Christian maturity. This is the goal of Christian education.

To say that by definition adolescence is a critical period is not to imply that all or most adolescents are in perpetual turmoil and rebellion. A major difficulty faced by teachers is the tendency of many persons to use generalized labels and emotional arguments. Consider this excerpt from a letter to the editor of a daily newspaper.

> If an underage offspring goes out and gets sloppy drunk, [parents should] let the police put them [sic] in the drunk tank and let them [sic] sober up in their own puke. There is no way we can get drunken drivers off the road by mollycoddling them. Too many of today's parents do not have any control over their teenagers, so they just turn them loose on society and hope some organization will keep them from getting killed ... or from killing or injuring innocent people.

> Teenagers have not changed over the centuries; they have always been ornery at that age . . . .

Think of the effects this sort of stereotyping and labeling can have. Many adult readers may jump to the conclusion that most drunken drivers are teenagers, and that most teenagers get drunk. Furthermore, they may tend to accept the image of teenagers as "ornery."

The teenage readers may become angry, resentful, disrespectful of adults, and less likely to trust them. They may stereotype adults in the same way the writer stereotypes them. Adults who seek to teach and befriend young people must carry an extra burden of proving that they reject the image of adolescents as troublemakers. A barrier of mistrust and defensiveness must be overcome every time the teacher attempts to help students modify behavior, escape worldly pressures, and make appropriate choices.

This complex state of affairs is more common than most teachers realize. It illustrates aptly the need for deep insights and empathy, commitment to the teaching mission, personal integrity, and dependence upon the guidance of the Holy Spirit.

Adolescence: Definitions and Descriptions

Teacher training programs customarily include brief studies of general characteristics and typical behavior patterns of each age-group (or developmental stage). Optimum effectiveness in the use of teaching-learning processes requires that teachers of teenagers have additional preparation and background. The subject of adolescence should be considered from several distinctive viewpoints so that it is not perceived simplistically, as a problem or as a time of struggle. The teacher should have factual knowledge about not only adolescents' involvement in social problems, but also their involvement in Christian ministry and positive social actions. The confusion and turmoil of growing up should be seen as a concern, but no teacher should overlook the wondrous emergence of unique human beings.

ADOLESCENCE AS A DEVELOPMENTAL STAGE

Our perception of adolescence results more from social conditions than from the actual nature of human beings. And this
perception is reinforced by our cultural tendency to think in
terms of physical and psychological development. In societies
historically or geographically removed from our own, the period
of growing up and receiving education is not prolonged. Even
in our own country, between the rich and the poor are great
differences about the age their children must earn a living and
assume adult responsibilities.

Because of the economic and social conditions in our country
and the need to get more education, the period of dependence
has increased. At the same time, the life-style in our rapidly
developing industrialized and urbanized society has propelled
children into growing up. Possibly as a result of better nutrition
children reach puberty at an early age; thus early adolescence,
or pubescence, may begin at 10. What is generally called middle
adolescence is from about 14 to about 18 years; and later adolescence, or youth, may extend from about 17 through the
early 20s.

EARLY ADOLESCENCE

The most dramatic biological changes of life seem to come
suddenly, although in fact the process is gradual. The usual
sequence is for a spurt of growth to be followed by increasingly
obvious sexual changes. The body changes shape; hair appears
in new places; the boy's voice cracks; the girl must master new
skills related to the menstrual cycle. Both males and females
may have skin problems, body odors, and other grooming needs
that demand new kinds of behavior.

Girls generally mature earlier than boys, and some individuals of both sexes mature much more rapidly than others. This
difference in the rate of maturation is the basis for one of the
first concerns of adolescence. Girls may be embarrassed by early
development, or upset because their development is slow. Boys
whose growth is slow often feel inadequate and left out. Thus

the earliest physical changes begin to have social and psychological consequences as the young people compare themselves with others and become self-critical and anxious.

MIDDLE ADOLESCENCE

While early adolescence is characterized by biological changes, the critical aspects of middle adolescence are related to mental, emotional, and social factors. Behavior at this stage may be perceived from two viewpoints: (1) breaking away from family ties, and (2) becoming attached to a peer group. Whereas the young person seeks independence and strives to adapt to himself as a new identity, his individualism is modified by his social inclinations. He may believe that he is doing his own thing, when in reality he is following peer leadership. At this point teachers need to understand, and help adolescents understand, that the turmoil they feel does not result entirely from biological stresses or unhappy relationships with parents. The frustration and discomfort come from the teenager's conflicting values and his attempts to reconcile the many contradictory elements of his life.

For example, parents and relatives may tell of their early struggles and triumphs, and yet expect young people to accept passive and obedient roles. Some youths express the opinion that they would like to be trusted to make their own way, as their parents did. On the other hand, the young have a world very different from that of many parents. They have the freedom and privacy that comes from driving a car. They are faced with the availability of drugs and alcohol. What the parents call self-control is not a social value today. "Falling into temptation" is likely to be viewed by the peer group as doing what is natural and being an authentic person.

The young person at this stage is struggling for independence, being pulled one way by his parents and another way by his peers. It is no wonder that he seems to alternate between extreme states—one moment enthusiastic and the next withdrawn and moody, one moment filled with idealistic intentions and the next ready to indulge his basest impulses. The middle adolescent seems to demand attention, and yet resents the well-meant interest of parents and teachers.

LATE ADOLESCENCE

By the time of graduation from high school most young persons are ready to resist pressures from both parents and peers, and make their own decisions. During this period issues concerning marriage and career become critical. Choices in these areas will have enduring consequences. And answers to the three main "life questions" of *identity, personal relationships,* and *value system* (or philosophy) are greatly affected now by every choice that is made.

Most young persons are aware that this is a period of important decisionmaking, and they articulate in some manner the following questions:

1. Who am I? How can I be myself?
2. How do I relate to others? What is my responsibility in establishing relationships?
3. What is really important? What do I really want?
4. What do I believe? What is the basis for my belief?

Those who teach and counsel youth must be especially alert to hear these questions because they may not be asked in direct form. Any opportunity to discuss such issues as part of a lesson presentation should be recognized and utilized.

It is generally accepted that the basic element in adolescent trauma and turmoil is the search for identity. Developmental psychologists say that in order to be ready for adulthood the adolescent must achieve a sense of self, or "ego identity." The identity crisis is at its peak in adolescence. During this time young people may experiment with various roles in an effort to find themselves. They want to be sure that their decisions are their own and not pressed upon them. Their confusion and uncertainty may lead to behavior that is labeled delinquent or rebellious. They test extremes in order to discover for themselves what is genuine, but most of them sincerely desire stability and truth. If they are given appropriate guidance at this point and, at the same time, allowed some freedom to experiment, most of them will achieve the sense of self needed to establish satisfactory relationships and make meaningful choices.

For modern youth, the matters of identity and relationship may be more complex than for previous generations because of changing sex role concepts. Whether to plan for marriage or a single life-style, whether to plan for children or no children, whether to put self-development and career before family concerns—these are questions common to adolescents today that may never have been considered by their parents.

From the Viewpoint of Social Problems

Those who treat the subject of adolescent turmoil in textbooks on social problems use two main approaches: (1) youth alienation and contraculture or subculture, and (2) juvenile delinquency and crime.

The youth subculture is said to be characterized by the rejection of conventional social values, as young people perceive them. For example, the adult world is accused of materialism and hypocrisy, and the youth culture is built upon values such as naturalness, authenticity, personal freedom, spontaneous expression, and immediate gratification of desires. These values can lead to indulgence in drugs, alcohol, sexual liberties, and emphasis upon pleasure-seeking as opposed to the work ethic of the older generations. The results of these activities can include addiction, pregnancies, venereal diseases, and crime.

Juvenile delinquency and crime are matters of great concern in our society, and in almost every part of the world today. In 1981, juveniles were involved in thirty-nine percent of all arrests for murder, rape, robbery, motor vehicle thefts, and arson. Juveniles are also involved in drug sales, prostitution, and other illegal behaviors.

A very serious problem in our society is teenage pregnancies.

We noted in chapter 3 that rebellion or a desire to escape home conditions, as well as sexual impulses, lead girls to have babies. The lasting effects upon the girl, the baby, and the society make this a problem that demands attention from all who work with adolescents.

Psychologists describe the involvement of adolescents in contraculture and delinquency as "acting out" behaviors. Supported by a gang or his peer group, the teenager tries to assert independence and gain acceptance by others. He is trying to act out an adult role, and gain a sense of power by beating the system.

Another social problem treated in most textbooks is runaway youth. Annually over 730,000 youths run away for at least one night.[1] This "running from" behavior indicates frustration, inability to communicate with parents, and sometimes the feeling of rejection after disputes with family members or friends. The ultimate "running from" behavior is suicide. The fact that suicide has become a leading cause of death among adolescents indicates the seriousness of their need.

The Christian teacher must understand that when adolescents are involved in social problems, it is not merely an indication that they are rebellious and "ornery at that age," as the unthinking citizen declared. It may mean that people who are confused and hurt are trying to act out their feelings or run away from situations. And uninformed teachers may actually contribute to such behavior. In their eagerness to teach young people the concepts of delayed gratification and submission to authority, teachers sometimes actually lay the foundation for rebellion against conventional attitudes and values. Too much emphasis upon being submissive and working hard for a future reward makes adolescents feel that the present is constricting, their needs and motives are not understood, their worth as persons is not recognized. Teachers should emphasize the positive values and joys of Christian living. They should provide youth with opportunities for acting out their problems and needs in a constructive manner. In a climate of acceptance the adolescent may feel free to express feelings, ideas, and opinions in spontaneous and authentic ways, thus dissolving the basis for alienation and rebellion.

SOCIAL SERVICE AND ALTRUISM

When the relationships of adolescents in the society are discussed, the tendency is to dwell upon conflicts and negative behaviors. However, teenagers are very much involved in making positive contributions to the society. They are among the most enthusiastic and productive workers in the church and in all types of helping activities.

Studies indicate that altruism develops as a combination of thinking and feeling. Adolescents recognize that others have personality structures and emotions similar to their own. They project or transfer their feelings and needs to others and become aware of the types of needs they might help to meet.

Most young people are sympathetic with the plight of individuals in distress, with groups who are poor, oppressed, or victimized in some way, and they are willing to get involved for service.

Ironically, adults sometimes misinterpret altruism, and think that young people are too liberal or rebellious when they show interest in reform movements and social causes. Instead of ignoring social issues, the wise teacher will use them to direct the altruistic tendencies of the students into constructive channels. Adolescents, like persons of all ages, often find that their own situation becomes less bothersome as they turn their attention to the needs of others. Recognizing and appealing to the positive strengths of teenagers may be more effective than trying to supply them with solutions for their own problems.

From the Viewpoint of the Generation Gap

Sunday school leaders have said for years what experts in crisis management are beginning now to say: "Optimum effectiveness in reaching a child or young person requires some knowledge of the home and family situation. Psychology and education are dependent upon understanding the social context that influences each client or student." This means that unless teachers are aware of teen-family relations, they are being unrealistic, and probably will come across to the students as naive.

Parents, as well as teachers, tend to treat the trauma of adolescence as though it is something that happened suddenly. Parents may say they are living with strangers. The implication is that the adolescent is some new kind of person. But people are not actually members of categories. Each one is a total person, passing through the various stages of life. The parents who do not know their teenagers may never have developed a true acquaintance with them as children. They perceived them as a category: children—expected to obey parents, be fed and clothed, go to school, and so forth. They were not exactly people to be *known.* But one day the parent is made very much aware of a nearly grown-up person. That person seems like a stranger, and the parent feels puzzled or even hurt.

Many parents overreact to their teenagers. They are very anxious to see them succeed (as parents define success), and show their approval of every small achievement. But they become intensely critical when they feel let down or disappointed by the behavior of their offspring.

It is common for teenagers to respond with complete misunderstanding of the parents' attitude. The teen does not see that the parent has sincere and justifiable concern. "My folks think they have some big investment in me," one young man complained. "I'm supposed to turn out right so they'll get a fair return and not be embarrassed. They don't see me as a person, but as a product."

The parents complain that the son or daughter is disrespectful, unappreciative, irresponsible. Some parents confess that they are repulsed by the behavior of their teenagers. They were brought up to be neat, and now they are messy and destructive. They insist on playing noisy tapes and filling the house with crude strangers.

The term *generation gap* has worldwide usage and has been

of interest to writers and social scientists for many years. Recent scholarly works on the subject have resulted in a classification of generational differences that can result in confusion and conflict. Four main concepts derived from this literature may be summarized as follows:[2]

1. Some conflict is inevitable since social structures and values change from generation to generation. Adolescents live in a different world than their parents did. The present influences of the automobile, television, and styles of music are typical examples of this "different world." Other examples are changing attitudes toward sex that, for example, allow males and females to share college residence facilities; permissiveness in dress (wearing jeans in church, for example); acceptance of attendance at movies. The influence of this environment makes the teenager different in ways the older generation cannot fully understand.

2. Some rebellion is normal and inevitable as young people struggle to become independent. In order to establish their identity, they feel almost compelled to disagree with their elders. Some have admitted that they have periods when they would disagree with *anything* a parent said. This type of rebellion is not based upon genuine value changes. It is simply the difference between age-groups, and when the young are mature they will return to most of the values they rejected.

3. Basic values may be expressed in different ways, so what is seen, for example, as hypocrisy by a teenager may be viewed as diplomacy by the elders.

4. Social change affects everyone in the population, not just the young. Therefore, older persons are struggling with their own values and making their own adaptations while trying to maintain norms for their children and encourage the younger generation to respect conventional customs and values. As a result, older persons may become self-conscious and defensive.

Spiritual and Moral Development

For the Christian teacher, the most important fact about

adolescence is that it is the stage of major spiritual and moral development. Experiences and decisions in this period will strongly influence, or even completely determine, the entire future of the individual.

Teaching can be made more effective if the teacher understands something of how adolescents reason and think about spiritual and ethical matters. Although we think of religion as being concerned with the emotions, studies of moral and spiritual development in the teen years clearly indicate that cognitive processes are closely related to the acceptance or rejection of the church and the establishment of personal beliefs.

The theories of response to social influence are useful here. According to these theories, the lowest level of response is *compliance,* in submission to authority, or to avoid pain or receive pleasure. The highest level of response is *internalization,* a principle-oriented action motivated by personal belief.

Much of the teaching in Sunday school requires a kind of compliance response. Truths are presented and students are expected to accept them on the basis of authority. When teenagers begin to object and question, such behavior may be labeled rebellious. In reality it may be an indication that the young people are developing the ability to think about the issues. By no means should this be considered a problem. The ability to think is the critical point of real decisionmaking and value formation, which is the real purpose of Christian education.

Eventually, under the guidance of the Holy Spirit, and the direction of skilled teachers, the young person will accept the truth. But it will be by his own decision. It will be *internalized.* It will not be a concrete rule to follow but a principle to be observed. People who accept rules and do not reason are easily led into error, so the tendency of the teenager to reject rules and demand meaningful applications becomes an asset to the wise and loving teacher.

Practical Suggestions

FOR TEACHERS OF ADOLESCENTS

The key idea in all the best literature concerning work with teenagers is *give them room to grow.* Listen to them. Let them discuss real problems and their own ideas. Do not preach and criticize. Teens respect wisdom and proficiency, but they cannot be forced by authoritarian methods. They are sensitive to the moving of the Holy Spirit and are interested in Biblical truth presented simply. Therefore the teacher should not try to moralize, but allow the Spirit to apply the Word. Trust them to learn. Expect the best from them.

Teachers should not try to act like a teenager and use teen talk. Do not claim to "understand" them. They may complain that you don't understand them—but usually they prefer it that way.

FOR TEACHERS OF CHILDREN

Some adolescent psychologists say that by the time teenagers have really serious problems, it is almost too late to solve them. The best cure is prevention. At each stage in life a person must develop the ability to enter successfully into the next stage.

Be open with children. Talk to them about growing up when the subject arises naturally or when it can be brought into the lesson in appropriate ways. Listen. Answer questions simply and truthfully.

Invite some teenagers to help with class activities occasionally. The teens can participate in some fun times, such as teaching games or songs, or presenting a musical program to the children. This time together gives the children opportunity to be with good teen role models.

FOR TEACHERS OF ADULTS

If teenagers have become a subculture, it is partly because the society and the church have kept the age-groups isolated from one another. Teenagers spend so much time with members of their own age-group that it is not surprising their values and customs are drawn from peers.

The subject of relationships with adolescents should be discussed in all the adult groups. Young adults should be encouraged to be accepting of, and helpful to, teens, rather than being cynical of them, labeling and teasing them. Older adults are interested in the activities of the young. They should be helped to understand the adolescent behavior that puzzles or frightens them. Invite representatives of the teen classes to present features and give testimonies before the adult classes. Teens may provide music, arrange for transportation for the elderly, and help in other activities, such as hospital visitation.

Parents of adolescents can be greatly helped and supported by a Sunday school teacher who is aware of their needs and concerns. Drugs, alcohol, accidents, sexual activities, and inappropriate companions of their children worry most parents. Sometimes they are pressed financially in trying to keep up with the needs and desires of their children. Because of troubles in the family, sometimes parents are angry and hurt; other times they feel guilty and frightened.

Provide opportunities for discussion of these matters in the adult classes. Emphasize to parents that in spite of outside influences, the teachings and examples in the home are very powerful. Most teenagers eventually become reconciled with their parents and follow the wishes of their families in areas of major importance.

Summary

Many of the problems faced by teens are attributable to change: change in social values, growth changes, emotional highs and lows, changes in expected behavior (especially in American culture where no definite age or accomplishment determines adulthood). In his struggle to become independent and establish identity, the teenager often seems rebellious, defiant, and disrespectful of adults and their values.

Teachers must be aware of the typical behavior patterns in

the developmental stages of early, middle, and late adolescence. Using this insight with love and empathy, the teacher can overcome the generation gap and guide his students in their choices and their commitment to God.

NOTES

[1]Michael S. Bassis and R. Gelles, *Social Problems,* ed. by Robert K. Merton (New York: Harcourt, Brace, Jovanovich, Inc., 1982).

[2]Vern L. Bengtson, "The Generation Gap," *Issues in Adolescent Psychology,* Dorothy Rogers, ed. (New York: Appleton-Century-Crofts, 1972).

5

The Mid-Life Crisis

Speaking the truth in love, we will in all things grow up into him. . . . The whole body . . . grows and builds itself up in love, as each part does its work (Ephesians 4:15,16).

"When I was a child, I spoke, understood, and thought as a child: but when I became an adult, I could never think as a child anymore, because my understanding was transformed by love." This is my paraphrased summation of Paul's magnificent declaration in 1 Corinthians 13. Within this chapter maturity and love come very close to being synonymous concepts. Notice how they are related again in Paul's letter to the Ephesians: "Until we all . . . become mature, attaining to the whole measure of the fullness of Christ . . . no longer infants. . . . Instead, speaking the truth in love, we will in all things grow up into him who is the Head, that is, Christ" (Ephesians 4:13-15).

Perhaps partly as a reflection of the youth-oriented society today, maturity seems to be little valued in our church culture. Sometimes we take pride in needing the milk of childhood rather than accepting the strong meat of responsible maturity. Consider, for example, the song that begs the Lord for a "brand new touch" because the "strength of yesterday is gone." By this reasoning, real Christian development would be neither expected nor encouraged.

Certainly we are promised strength on a daily basis, and we must acknowledge continually our dependence upon the Lord. Nevertheless, the church must expect and encourage its people to mature. The church must provide a structure by which believers become progressively stronger and more loving. The power that casts out the fear of aging is love. The serenity and wisdom that acknowledge change and accept the challenge of each new phase of life come from growing up into Him in all things and speaking the truth in love.

Even though relatively new terms such as adolescence and mid-life crisis can hardly be expected to appear in the Bible, life span issues do. The Bible gives much attention to age-oriented relationships and responsibilities among individuals, families, and generations. It might be said that a suggestion of what Robert Havighurst proposes as developmental task theory can be detected throughout the Bible.[1] His approach to understanding human development perceives a lifelong process in stages, including the "tasks" typically accomplished at each stage of life. Achievement of each task brings a degree of strength and satisfaction to individuals and prepares them to be successful in future stages of life.

Havighurst's Developmental Tasks
Ages 30-55

1. Achieve adult social and civic responsibility
2. Establish and maintain an appropriate standard of living
3. Help teenage children become happy and responsible adults
4. Develop worthwhile adult leisure activities
5. Relate adequately to the spouse as a person
6. Accept and adapt to the physical changes of middle life
7. Adjust to aging parents[2]

Obviously each item on the list does not apply to every individual. Items three and five can be modified to include responsibilities that unmarried persons have to families and friends.

In spite of its limitations, Havighurst's view of the life span is more compatible with Scripture than are most of the popular writings that place so much emphasis upon personal crisis and personal gratification. The Bible assumes that God's people will accept responsibility, teach and provide for future generations, and look upon their lives as integrated with His purpose and plan for all humanity. (See 1 Peter 4:10; 2 Timothy 2:1-10.) Popular writings, on the other hand, usually assume that people have no stable idea of purpose for their lives, that self-love is more important than love for others, and that feeling obligated to people or causes is a weakness. Most of the popular literature is written from the viewpoint of life without God. Nevertheless, we can learn much from excellent scholars who have studied and written about the life span. We shall consider a few concepts that are especially helpful to Christian teachers.

1. *Life is a constant movement with overlapping stages.* This means that a student is never simply *in* a class, but is moving through. Some writers prefer the term *life course,* rather than life span or life cycle. Certainly the apostle Paul thought of his life as a course, a race, a journey filled with adventures, changes, perils, and tasks (see, e.g., 2 Timothy 4:6,7).

2. *Transition periods between stages are called crises*—not in the sense of disasters and problems but as turning points or significant events that cause questioning and adjustments. The mid-life crisis is seen by some as an opportunity for evaluation and mid-course correction (see, e.g., John 16:33 and Ecclesiastes 2:1-25).

3. *Everyone experiences similar stages at different rates.* Males and females move through the same or very similar stages, but their rates of movement may differ. This factor is involved in many misunderstandings and conflicts between the sexes. It is a fact the teacher should keep in mind in making scriptural applications.

4. *Responses to crisis stages are relatively predictable.* Personality traits have some effect upon the responses of individuals, but usually the response tendencies associated with the crisis points are relatively predictable. Therefore, teachers can help people anticipate how they may feel and help them make preparations. When an individual knows in advance what to

expect, he is in a much better position to control his behavior and make appropriate adjustments.

5. *General predictability is modified by the social situation and the environment.* It is important for teachers to keep this in mind and emphasize it to the students. We operate in a Christian environment. Therefore, we are not compelled to accept as "normal" whatever the world believes about human behavior. We are not conformed to the world's notions, but are transformed by the renewing of our minds (Romans 12:2). For example, writings on stress and burn-out tend to be fatalistic and earth-centered. People get tired and discouraged and sometimes think they are worthless or not appreciated, but Paul kept racing ahead because he was sure of a worthwhile goal (Hebrews 12:1,2; Romans 8:18-21). Paul never lost his enthusiasm for a good cause, and there is no reason to believe that it is inevitable for us to do so at mid-life or any time.

6. *Both biological and emotional functions affect response.* The life stages are associated with biological functions, but the response of the individual is not absolutely determined by biological changes. Personal perception and interpretation often overcome physical factors. Again we have an indication of the effects good teaching can have. Even when matters such as hormones and changing body contours are involved, the power of the Holy Spirit is available to help the Christian adapt.

Definition and Background

The idea that something happens at mid-life that is similar to adolescence and more dramatic than mere gradual aging was introduced into psychological literature only a few years ago. Some credit a British psychoanalyst, Elliott Jaques, with coining the term *mid-life crisis.* Current textbooks in developmental psychology describe mid-life crisis as "a critical period during middle age when an individual is induced by personal, physical, and social factors to examine his life. It may result in important modifications of life-style and philosophy."[3]

Some believe this postulated crisis has become a focus of attention because of increased longevity and affluence; people have more time and freedom to analyze their personal development. Also, most adults in our society are better educated than ever before, and they have access to television and periodicals, which stimulate interest in such matters. Smaller families and more options make it logical that people would be drawn to consider how they might change their employment, life-style, and educational attainment at mid-point in life while time and energy remain.

Critical unhappiness, stress, and disillusionment with life and work are found to be common among men in management and professional positions, and among women who have strong career ambitions. Most people are able to make gradual adjustments between their aspirations and their achievements, but those who do not may experience severe turmoil in mid-life. Because customs and values are so varied and are changing so rapidly in our society, an increasing number of people are likely to need help in making these adjustments. Two related examples of these social changes are the transitions in the concepts of sex roles and the increased rate of divorce and remarriage at the mid-life stage.

There must be a new sensitivity to the real needs and problems of those who attend our classes, and to the guidance of the Holy Spirit in making appropriate use of our educational tools. Competent classroom teachers will accept those who suffer, without assuming that all middle-aged people respond in the same way. Most of all, it must be remembered that any transition point is a possible doorway to new experiences with the Lord and spiritual growth. A class of supportive Christians led by a sensitive and proficient Bible teacher is the best environment for people who are making life-changing decisions.

With this in mind, the following descriptions and observations about the nature of the mid-life crisis will give the teacher a framework within which to prepare for instruction.

What Is the Mid-Life Crisis?

A GENERAL AWARENESS

The opening of Gail Sheehy's book *Passages* is only a little more dramatic than many other personal accounts of a sudden awareness experience in mid-life. Sheehy saw a young companion killed, and felt the brush of a bullet pass her own face. The awesome truth of her finitude and vulnerability led her to realize that, even without violence, life is uncertain and short. At first she was frightened. Then she thought she was going mad. Then she began to question life's meaning and evaluate her priorities. Finally, she decided to turn from less important pursuits and do something that to her was really meaningful.[4]

Similar awareness experiences, sudden or gradual, mark for many individuals the onset of mid-life. Some people believe they are cracking up, or having a nervous breakdown. They question their values. They go through emotions of rage, resentment, regret, disillusionment; they lose their temper, blame their spouses or their work, feel victimized, say they are burned-out, and want to run away from everything.

The peak years of responses of this sort are from about 37 to 45. Before this point, people have been deeply involved with careers or rearing children. They have not really thought about death. They are interested in achievement, and what they do seems to be the necessary, inevitable pattern they are supposed to follow.

The awareness experience changes this. Middle-aged people may ask, "Why am I doing all this?" "Is this all there is to life?" "What do I really believe and desire?" "Am I being my real self?" "Do I want to keep on like this for the rest of my life?" These people often feel what Sheehy calls the deadline, generating thoughts of *I'm not getting any younger—if I want to do anything different, I'd better get started.*[5]

For most men, anxiety is focused first on their work. They may realize that they will never reach their goals. Or they may decide that their efforts have been meaningless. They wonder what course can be taken now before it is too late. For married women the deadline may concern the question of whether or not to go on with the marriage, have one more child, go back to school, or look for employment. Single women face deadlines, too. Should they struggle ahead in their present work? Should they change jobs, get more education, move to a location where conditions are possibly better for finding a marriage partner?

PHYSICAL AND EMOTIONAL CRISES AT MID-LIFE

For most individuals some physical changes at middle age are obvious. The body changes shape. Usually there is a weight gain. Men lose hair. Vision is affected, and eyeglasses are necessary for many people. There is a general slowdown, a tired feeling, vague pains and sometimes frightening symptoms. For all this, not nearly as much change occurs as is generally feared. Slowdown in speed does not mean loss in accuracy in most activities. Sense perceptions—colors, tastes, and smells—remain adequate. Well-educated people show little or no decline in performance. Hormonal changes do not automatically lead to problems. Those who are aware of what to expect and have learned to cope are able to adjust without undue distress to normal physical changes.

For most women, menopause occurs between the ages of 40-55. The most common complaints are hot and cold sensations, and depression. Only about 10 percent of all women are obviously inconvenienced in any way. Sex life is not impaired, and indeed is likely to become more satisfactory for many.

The so-called men's menopause (or climacteric) seems to affect significantly only about 15 percent of males. Men have not been taught, as have women, to know what to expect, so many react in panic. Partly because some men have used menopause as an argument against having women in responsible career positions, the idea of male menopause is abhorrent to them. Consequently severe emotional problems may result when they have the experience. The average age of the men who seek medical help for climacteric symptoms is 53.7 years. The symptoms are caused by hormonal variations, and include unpredictable changes of mood, sweats, chills, morning fatigue, lassitude, and vague pains. Impotence before the age of 65 is rarely associated with hormones, but is usually psychological in origin. Marriage problems in mid-life may occur because women past the child bearing stage often enjoy sexual activity more than they did previously. The husband may have diminished desires and capabilities at this age.

SOME TYPICAL RESPONSES

Some people respond to middle age changes with behaviors that may be compared to the grief process. The first stage is denial, in which people try to prove to themselves and others that they are still young. They select youthful clothing and try to act young. They may be obsessed with diet and physical fitness programs. They get hair pieces or transplants, use hair color, and get stylish haircuts. They may have affairs to prove they are attractive. More women engage in extramarital sex between the ages of 36 and 40 than at any other age.

After the denial stage may come anger, when people become bitter and resentful, blaming others for their condition. Spouses often blame each other for lost opportunities and the failure of their dreams to come true. They may blame the marriage to the point that they separate or divorce. Single persons blame the job, society, discrimination, the opposite sex, or the church.

A third stage is depression. Some people become acutely aware of the ages of those listed in the obituary column. They become obsessively afraid of cancer and develop hypochondria. During extreme depression they may indulge in self-destructive acts, such as alcohol or drug abuse, careless driving, and even suicide. Suicide rates increase at this time of life, especially for men aged 55-65.

Most persons finally achieve acceptance. This attitude need not be viewed as apathy, or interpreted as failure. It can be a genuine acceptance of self as a middle-aged person with a recognition of the positive aspects of being this age. People should find a renewal at this point and make truly happy adjustments while they have the energy to enjoy the golden years of life.

Work and the Mid-Life Crisis

Invariably a child will be asked, "What do you want to be?"

From that moment identity becomes more and more attached to a vocation, until the vocation comes to be the measure of personal worth. College education today is oriented almost entirely toward careers. Women, as well as men, are convinced that their identity and their happiness depend upon vocational success. They look to work not only for material gain, but for status, social acceptance, and self-esteem.

For many people a time comes when the career seems more like a losing battle than a challenging occupation. Some individuals feel panic. Time is running out. Some are resentful and angry. Others feel personally inadequate and ready to give up. Even persons who are considered very successful suffer disillusionment. Work loses its meaning. Suddenly they wonder if work has been worth the time and effort given to it for so many years. Some experience what is called burn-out, a point of physical and emotional fatigue where the zest for work is lost and everything seems futile.

Complications in Home Life

At the same time a man feels driven or disillusioned in his work situation, his wife may be dissatisfied with her role in the home. She is unable to provide the comfort the man needs, and he is unable to understand her discontent. Perhaps the children are leaving, and she feels depressed and useless. The "empty nest" experience affects women more than men, because more of the man's satisfactions have come from outside the home. In many cases couples have not learned to communicate, so each remains puzzled, or even angered by the behavior of the other.

A considerable amount of material has been written about the "empty nest," but a crowded or refilled nest may be even more distressful. Grown children do not always leave. If they remain, new roles must be defined for every member of the household. The parents are no longer in charge of children, but the young people are limited by the need to harmonize their lives with that of the parents. Relationships, responsibilities, and privileges must be worked out in order to avoid tension and conflict.

Sometimes grown children leave and then return, bringing problems with them. Given the increasing sexual liberties and the divorce rate, it is to be expected that some grown children will return with children of their own. Middle-aged parents may find themselves in these situations at a point when they were beginning to think of some relaxation or pursuit of new interests. They may be torn between feelings of resentment and feelings of obligation.

A most painful decision at middle age may be what to do about elderly parents. If they are brought into the household many adjustments must be made. Arguments and resentments may arise among siblings over financial arrangements or other responsibilities in the care of their parents.

What the Teacher Can Do

Havighurst points out that the dissatisfactions associated with middle age are symptoms of a lack of success in the areas of the developmental tasks. If a way is found to accomplish the tasks, then satisfaction results. He believes that the church should help its members accomplish their developmental tasks in religious ways. If a person can be guided toward success in the religious dimension of a task, his value system and perspective will be modified so that worldly values will not control his ambitions. The need for achievement is not eliminated by Christianity, but in Christ, achievement takes on a new meaning.[6]

The teacher who knows what the needs and tasks are has a tremendous advantage. Parents can be given specific help in dealing with teenagers. Adults can be encouraged to respect the needs of their spouses, and adjust to aging parents in ways specifically outlined and illustrated in the Word of God. (See Titus 2:4,5; Colossians 3:15-21; 2 Timothy 1:5.) If class members do require formal counseling, the informed teacher will be able to recognize this and take appropriate steps. The work of the pastor or other counselors will be facilitated when the client has the knowledge of scriptural principles upon which to build.

Christian teachers should be aware that most of the non-Christian self-help books and popular works are written from the viewpoint of nonreligious existentialism. That is, they advocate development of self-esteem and personal identity as the highest possible goal. Gail Sheehy, in her book *Passages*, declares that the only way to make a satisfactory adjustment to life and other people is to establish self-sufficiency and aloneness.[7] Assertiveness and willingness to abandon all relationships, even marriage, in order to acquire true personhood are major values in most of these writings. The non-Christian existentialist believes that the greatest courage is to be able to believe in nothing and depend on no one. The liberated person is supposed to build all relationships on his or her own terms, and refuse to remain involved in any relationship that does not give full satisfaction.

It is obvious that the positive quality of being true to oneself is distorted in these writings. Readers get the impression that divorce is a virtue, self-indulgence is courage, and religion is a childish dependency.

Practical Suggestions

Accept all persons in love, but do not excuse self-seeking and abandonment of responsibility.

Emphasize love in Biblical terms by reading the passages on love during lesson presentations.

Emphasize the fruit of the Spirit, the joy of developing Christian maturity, the need to be loving and forgiving.

Express compassion for all peoples and races. Involve the class in missionary projects. Show the need to feel responsible for the welfare of others in the community and the world.

Do not be judgmental or condemning, but speak out plainly concerning sin and worldly values. Encourage free and honest discussion and listen to the ideas and opinions from students.

Do not try to teach people how to develop self-worth. Give them examples that prove the church cares about them—that you respect and trust them. Self-worth cannot be developed by an individual from within himself. It must be acquired from relationships with God and from caring people.

"Love your neighbor as yourself" does not mean you must love yourself in a self-conscious way before you can love others. It means you should love your neighbor with the same quality of love as you have for yourself. If you care enough to feed, groom, and educate yourself, then you can care about others.

Help people get acquainted with one another and develop happy relationships. The class members need social experiences with one another.

Emphasize the two major concepts that determine successful middle age: Acceptance of self and the maintenance of satisfactory relationships.

For Teachers of Those Below Middle Age

Anticipation of, and education about, what lies ahead in the normal growth and development of your students will help resolve the crises they will face. Foundations for self-esteem and love and respect of people must be laid in childhood.

Emphasize relationships between groups of various types. Use the word *people* instead of *children* to help children develop the concept that they are one with other ages, different only in degree—not kind.

Educators are reevaluating the abandonment of traditional virtues of respect for authority and courteous behavior. Instill them.

Acquaint adolescents with the prospects of maturing and the relationship between generations and life stages. Adolescents can learn empathy for older people through roleplay, simulation games, field trips, and guest speakers addressing how to cope with one or the other of life's stages.

Use positive references to middle age and senior adulthood. Remember, you are educating them for living life—all of it.

Summary

Many people experience turmoil at mid-life if they are unable to make adjustments between their dreams and the realities of their achievements. They experience feelings of regret, disillusionment, burn-out, and want to run away from everything—marriage, career, and familiar life-styles.

The accomplishment of developmental tasks at each stage of life brings strength and satisfaction to people. The teacher should encourage free and honest discussion, and express compassion, at the same time speaking out against self-seeking and abandonment of responsibility. Involve the class in the welfare of others, emphasize the fruit of the Spirit, and the joy of developing Christian maturity.

NOTES

[1]Robert J. Havighurst, *Developmental Tasks and Education* (New York: McKay, 1972).

[2]*Ibid.*

[3]Dorothy Rogers, *The Adult Years: An Introduction to Aging* (Englewood Cliffs, NJ: Prentice-Hall, 1982).

[4]Gail Sheehy, *Passages* (New York: Bantam Books, Inc., 1979).

[5]*Ibid.*

[6]Havighurst, *Developmental Tasks.*

[7]Sheehy, *Passages.*

6

Illness

Listen closely to my words. . . . for they are life to those who find them and health to a man's whole body (Proverbs 4:20,22).

Modern science runs panting along behind the Bible, sometimes almost touching its truth. A number of doctors and researchers in the medical field are talking today of a "new" concept in which inner peace is a factor in healing. There is widespread interest in wholistic approaches, or holism, a concept of the person as a whole rather than as so many different fields of study, according to his disorder. Thus besides including anatomy, physiology, chemistry, and genetics, the holistic approach considers an individual's *internalized socialization* process. This refers to all that has become a part of the person from his environment and relationships: Language, beliefs, knowledge, habits, attitudes, ways of perceiving and responding to his world.

According to the holistic approach to healing, most, if not all, illness is related in some way to the emotions. Emotional stress influences the digestion, heartbeat, respiration, kidney function, hormone and enzyme production—indeed all bodily functions. Therefore, therapy must include some method of helping the patient to develop inner peace. Seminars and conferences are offered to teach people how to use the imagination to think happy, pleasant thoughts and resolve conflicts between their thoughts and feelings. The advertisement for one of these seminars says that students will be shown how to develop "a deep inner calmness . . . and maximize health and vigor."

A modern medical doctor says, "Healing begins from inner peace, from which flow joy, wonder and a sense of awe." He is not very far from discovering truth. The Sunday school teacher has the opportunity to help people resolve conflicts by teaching the source of that inner peace.

> The Lord is near. Do not be anxious about anything, but . . . present your requests to God. And the peace of God, which transcends all understanding, will guard your hearts and minds in Christ Jesus. . . . Whatever is true, whatever is noble, whatever is right, whatever is pure, whatever is lovely, whatever is admirable . . . think about such things. Whatever you have learned . . . put it into practice. And the God of peace will be with you (Philippians 4:5-9).

The anthropologist/philosopher Ashley Montagu declared that scientists have rediscovered that love is the road that leads to health and happiness. They "are giving a scientific foundation or validation to the Sermon on the Mount and to the Golden Rule,"[1] he wrote. Actually, it is the Bible which gives foundation or validation to the work of some diligent and intelligent scholars who have looked for truth by making astute observations of God's creation. Christian teachers need to take advantage of this exciting situation by combining references to both science and the Word to promote the mental and physical well-being of their students. Montagu's prescription for health and happiness? Love and relatedness. The condition of a person's health depends to some extent upon the quality of his relationships. People who are loved, love others, get along well, feel accepted, like to be friendly, seldom criticize others—in short, have good relationships—are likely to enjoy better health and be able to cope better with illness than those whose relationships are unhappy. Of course, the Christian teacher will emphasize the most important relationship—the one with the Lord Jesus Christ, the Prince of Peace.

The literature on holistic medicine carries other facts and ideas of great value to teachers. One such idea often overlooked is that health is greatly affected by life situations and environment. When someone comes home with a headache after "a hard day at work," the pain is seldom caused by a biological condition. Every aspect of the work situation (economic factors, events involving inanimate objects, such as machines) affects physical health.

Another pertinent fact is that guilt-producing behavior affects body functions and chemistry. It has been claimed that lung cancer may be related to the stress caused by the guilt over smoking, as well as to the carcinogenic elements in the smoke. This author believes there is a definite link between guilt and proneness to accidents.

How Shall They Hear Without a Teacher?

Most people do not automatically connect Bible readings and sermons in church with the healing needs of their bodies and minds unless such material refers specifically to healing. The teacher must frequently express the truth that peace and healing are available through Christ not only in healing services, but by reading and studying the Word and by daily Christian living. Consistent, positive Biblical teaching probably is more effective in meeting health needs than an occasional message on divine healing.

Religion Is Not an Instrument To Be Used

Since divine healing is the subject of official doctrinal positions in many religious organizations, the role of the teacher is critical. Students rely on the teacher for accurate interpretation of their church's statements, and for clarification of the fragments of information and ideas they encounter from time to time. Students must understand divine healing as a doctrine and not as an instrument to be applied in times of emergency.

The magic of backward societies is approached in this way, as an instrument to attain some end of the one who calls upon its supposed power. This should not be so of religion. A person who practices Christianity as religion receives benefits that are part of the whole experience and relationship with God.

Christianity is not a means for acquiring benefits, such as miracles of healing; it is an end in itself, in which the believer is made whole.

Probably most divine healing does not come in the form of miracles, as they are commonly understood. Healing comes as a natural consequence of God's love for those who trust and serve Him. It should be taught that healing is provided for in the atonement, and is the privilege of all believers. Students can be taught to pray for themselves and others. As they do they will see some obvious miracles. Also, they will enjoy the constant, quiet miracle of that inner peace that medical doctors now claim to be the most important source of physical and mental health.

Sickness, Health, and Healing in the Bible

Although some Christians have tended to put strong emphasis upon the difference between the natural and the spiritual, modern concepts of wholeness seem compatible with Biblical references to the human condition. Throughout the Scriptures much attention is given to matters of disease, sickness, concern for the physical needs of people, relationships between spiritual and physical conditions, and healing of the body. The *Thompson Chain-Reference Bible* assigns 37 categories to physical sickness and health, and lists over 150 references in these categories. Almost 20 percent of the writing in the Gospels is devoted to healing. Healing was a major part of the earthly ministry of Christ. The disciples were instructed in the matter of healing, and the apostles maintained this emphasis in the development of the church.

Throughout the Scriptures, obedience to God is related to health, and sin is related to sickness. Bodily affliction, undoubtedly, is a result of sin. But it does not follow that any one illness is the result of personal sin on the part of the sick person. Biblical examples connect illness with the emotions that are recognized as related to stress: jealousy, rebellion, discontent, coveteousness. Cheerfulness and positive thinking are related to good health.

Recent concern in the United States over major outbreaks of genital herpes and acquired immune deficiency syndrome (AIDS) has brought to public attention the old question of the relationship between sin and sickness. Public reports do not avoid the conclusion that the epidemics result from the "casual intimacies encouraged by the sexual revolution."[2]

At the same time, the media is very critical of anyone who suggests that the diseases are the result of sin. The position of the teacher should be that it is not a question of God's judgment upon an individual. We can declare with all authority from Scripture and from the evidence in our modern world that when God's laws are broken there are physical consequences. Thus we see again the interrelatedness of the spiritual and the physical—and that God, even more than modern medicine, is interested in the *whole* person.

How Illness Affects People

Reaction to illness varies greatly. Some experience minor pain in a major illness; others experience major pain in a minor illness. A person's attitude toward sickness results from past experiences or teachings. For example, some have been taught to believe that showing pain is a weakness, and some feel guilty, thinking all sickness is punishment. However, a number of reactions are typical of most sick people.

1. Fear is the most common emotion. There is fear of pain, fear that the illness is very serious and may result in death, and fear of disfigurement, as in the case of operations.

2. Anxiety is similar to fear, but the anxious uncertainties, such as waiting for laboratory reports, worrying about expenses and the loss of time on a job, add another dimension of fear.

3. Depression to some degree is felt by most sick people. It becomes serious when deep discouragement and self-pity lead to withdrawal and rejection of friendly gestures from others. Carried to the extreme it leads to the loss of interest in recovery or to suicide. Depression is always a matter for concern.

4. Anger is experienced by many who are sick. They may

feel just generally angry at themselves, the doctors, the family, and even the church and God. Frequently guilt and anger are associated. The person who is angry at himself becomes convinced that the illness is punishment for some act or neglect in the past.

5. Feelings of lack of control are experienced by most people who suffer illness or injury. Those who think of themselves as capable and independent suffer great frustration and embarrassment when they cannot regulate their own bodies. The fear of losing intellectual control is extremely threatening. Dependence upon others and admission of physical weakness is distressing.

The Attitude of the Teacher Is Important

How the teacher feels about sickness and sick people affects greatly the results of the teaching. The Bible records several accounts of godly people who were sick (2 Kings 13:14; Acts 9:37; 2 Timothy 4:20).[3] We are not to feel tense and helpless, or allow compassion to turn into pity. Most important, the teacher must be aware of the types of people in his class, and how they may be feeling, so that lesson material may be applied appropriately.

Hurting People in the Class

People with chronic illness and pain

Chronic sufferers need to be accepted. They may be grasping for meaning, asking, why? They need assurance. They may need to talk about their fears and worries. Although the teacher should give them opportunities to express themselves, he should firmly guide them away from self-pity. They should be kept involved in class activities to prove to themselves and others that they are capable of making worthwhile contributions.

If an illness is thought to be terminal, the person is likely to react according to the stages outlined by Dr. Kubler-Ross. (It was as a result of interviews with terminally ill persons that the stages were described originally.) The teacher who is aware of these stages has two advantages. First, appropriate support can be given to the student. Second, the teacher is not confused or alarmed, but understands what is happening and can be more comfortable and natural with the individuals.

People who have major handicaps

People who cannot see or walk, or have other obvious physical disabilities, require special thoughtfulness of the teacher. The tendency is for handicapped persons to become stigmatized. A stigma is a label that is used to characterize an individual, so he or she is not seen as a person but as a blind person, or a crippled person. Use of the word *blind* in a figurative sense is especially offensive to people who do not see.

Testimonies from handicapped individuals indicate that to feel really accepted into a group is a cherished experience for them. They in turn can be a great blessing to a group.

People who have sickness in the family

Studies of families in which one member is chronically ill show two opposite conditions. In some cases the strain of illness seems to precipitate family disintegration. A feeling of "living in the shadow of death" is reported by some. Family members may experience depression, interpersonal conflicts, and sometimes emotional illness. They may turn to drinking or drug abuse. Parents have feelings of failure, helplessness, and guilt. Brothers and sisters of sick children may feel neglected, jealous, and also guilty as they compete for attention. When the financial burden is overwhelming, the distress is even greater.

In other cases, researchers have reported amazing strength and family unity in times of adversity. Chronic illness brought family members closer together and resulted in the development of positive personality traits. The attitudes that make a difference between these two reactions seem to be a combination of maintaining a sense of hope, putting emphasis upon the worth of each person, and encouraging the sick one to transcend the infirmity. These studies make it clear that Christian teaching could have tremendous influence on the way a family responds to illness.

People who suffer from hypochondria

Hypochondriacs are people characterized by anxiety and unmet needs. Some people seem bitter and hostile, perhaps angry, and determined to get attention. Others are passive, withdrawn and pitiful, seeming to cling and beg for attention. All of them have found that sickness brings some benefits they are not able to gain in other ways. They do indeed experience physical symptoms and, although it is said that they enjoy being sick, their lives are not pleasant.

Perhaps teachers are better equipped than other types of helpers to give assistance to hypochondriacs. The basis of the condition is an unmet need, and Biblical instruction in a friendly group may meet that need. The first step for the teacher is to love and accept the student, and be free from the tendency to judge or scold. The next step is to help the student find satisfaction through mastery of the lesson material, interaction with the class members, and involvement in a service project. The goal is to help the student develop positive Christian qualities with the resultant feelings of meaning and self-worth. To be a healthy, active Christian will be more satisfying than to be sick, and the symptoms of physical illness will no longer have a place in his or her life.

People who minister to the sick

The Sunday school has a very special ministry to those who serve in the helping professions (such as nursing and social work) and for those who volunteer for hospital and home visitation. Sunday school is the place to come for spiritual refreshment, uniquely combined with the training needed to witness for Christ, pray for the sick, and encourage those who are depressed and exhausted by their own illness or that of loved ones. In a friendly, loving group, painful experiences of the past week can be shared, and happy triumphs reported so that all may rejoice together.

In our modern, complex society, burn-out among those who work with people in crises is much talked about. Professionals and volunteers get discouraged because of the multitudinous problems, their inability to help in many cases, and the stressful conditions imposed upon them. The Sunday school class provides a possible prevention of, and cure for, burn-out as the teacher stimulates lively interaction among interested and caring Christians. The joy and strength of the Christian professional can be renewed as he or she realizes the possibilities for service to Christ in the helping vocations.

Sick children

Another unique and often overlooked ministry of the Sunday school is to children who have serious chronic ailments. At a time when well children are learning to be independent and to fit into their social environment, the sick ones are deprived of opportunities for growth. The trial and error experiences that make children develop mentally and socially are denied sick children because of their physical condition. Being treated differently and prevented from joining in the activities of normal children make them lonely and self-conscious. They greatly need opportunities to experience success and a sense of belonging. A good Sunday school teacher can provide both by helping the child to participate in class activities, assume appropriate responsibilities, and accomplish concrete learning tasks that can be demonstrated to others.

Often sick children take upon themselves the burden of protecting their parents. They sense the unhappiness and frustration of their parents and are reluctant to add to the family problems by confiding their own feelings and needs. Frequently a nurse or teacher becomes a confidante. What a fine ministry for a Christian teacher, who has to offer not only the love and understanding of a person, but the greater love of God!

People with emotional and mental illnesses

Few people are aware of the magnitude of the mental health

problem in the United States. One in every eight men was rejected as psychologically unfit for military service under the selective service program, and since those figures were published, the number of those being treated for mental illness has risen steadily. Some of the characteristics of our society, such as rapid social change and widespread mobility, are the major causes of stress, which leads to breakdowns. People find themselves unable to adjust to the changing and inconsistent demands made upon them by different jobs, technologies, and value systems.

The resultant psychological disorder may be serious enough that a person loses touch with reality and becomes potentially dangerous *(psychosis)*. Or the disorder may be only a *neurosis*, characterized by anxieties, chronic physical complaints, and obsessive thoughts. However, the sufferer remains in touch with reality.

Although teachers are not usually counselors (and should not try to be), they can help the person experiencing neurosis— the category of mental illness they are most likely to meet— first, by caring enough to learn something about the person; second, by helping him to read, understand, and memorize Scripture; and, third, by providing positive social experiences. Furthermore, this person will frequently respond to Bible teaching, identifying with its characters and finding comfort in its promise of peace and healing.

Mental illness is easier to prevent than to cure. If people have the ability to love, work, and adjust to changes in their lives, they will be mentally healthy. Therefore, the best contribution a Christian teacher can make is to help people, beginning with the very young, to develop satisfactory adjustments, first to God, and then to people. Except for the grace of God, the effects of neglect in childhood teaching can never be completely overcome. On the other hand, the effects of good teaching and happy experiences in a Christian environment will overcome most of the threats to mental health throughout life.

People who may become ill

Almost everyone will suffer illnesses and injuries from time to time. Some who feel healthy now may discover soon that they have serious health problems. Such an experience will not be nearly so devastating when one has learned what the Bible says about sickness, and how to meet life's crises with Christian faith.

Perhaps the most effective way to teach the class (of whatever age-group) about pain and sickness is to bring out these issues naturally from the lesson material whenever it is appropriate. Then, when the subject arises, allow the group to ask questions and discuss freely their misgivings, fears, doubts, and confusion. Be ready to supplement your lesson material with specific Bible readings and information to fit the need. When a Bible lesson includes mention of a sick person, the class may spend some time in making an analysis of the situation. How is the sick person feeling? What is happening to family members? Can we put ourselves in their place? What would we do? How is the situation resolved? What can we learn about ourselves from this?

As the class members share their feelings and ideas, they learn to love and trust each other more. This helps them to build strength to face whatever comes, and to be better able to pray and help one another when critical needs arise in any of their lives.

The Meaning of Sickness

Sickness is a condition of being human in a fallen world. God gave man free will and made him subject to certain natural laws. The Bible teaches us that suffering has a place in our lives. It reminds us of our need for God, keeping us humble and conscious of our mortality. It helps us identify with the sufferings of Christ, and refines our character, making us more mature. It helps us to be patient and compassionate toward others.

"It was good for me to be afflicted" (Psalm 119:71). Often

when people suffer some affliction they become more aware of human limitations. They are able to slow down from a frantic, materialistic life and make realistic adjustments. They learn to appreciate the love of God and His people. They enjoy their families more. Life becomes generally more meaningful and satisfying.

Preparation To Face Sickness

The medical profession has recently become aware of the importance of patient education. Classes and seminars for diabetics, epileptics, heart patients, parents of sick children, and people who face surgery are held regularly. It has been discovered that people recover faster and experience less pain when they know what to expect.

We can apply the same principle to Christian education in relation to sickness. People need to develop attitudes and behaviors that will help them face problems and cope with crisis times. The Sunday school class can provide preparation for sickness by allowing opportunities for discussion of the fears and concerns involved.

The Question of Faith

Some people have been taught that it is always God's will to heal, so they blame themselves or judge others when healing does not come in answer to their prayers. They think that if only they had enough faith, healing would be granted. Some have been taught that God sets conditions for healing and that when all the conditions are met, healing will come. When healing is not evident, they believe that somehow a condition has not been met. If the class is conducted in a spirit of openness, such issues will arise and cannot be ignored. And there are no pat answers. What should the teacher do?

Be sure that the doctrinal position of the pastor is fully understood, and that literature is available for the use of the class members. Then point the class to the Word and pray that the Holy Spirit will guide application of the principles to the individual needs. Emphasis is upon meeting the need of students, not establishing specific dogma.

Summary

Everyone is subject to sickness, and it is not always a result of some personal failure or sin. Yet, a connection between spiritual and physical well-being does exist. To the question of why the righteous suffer, a statistician once answered, "When you look at the matter statistically, the righteous do escape suffering to a significant degree." That is, those behaviors that are called righteous are also those that lead to good health.

There is the obvious connection between sickness and substances that harm the body, such as tobacco, alcohol, and drugs. Misuse of sex leads to sickness. Indulgence in food and all excesses, such as fast driving, are harmful. Hate, anger, covetousness, and jealousy make people sick. On the other hand, good relationships with people help prevent illness. Those who love God and serve Him with gladness are less likely than the general population to become sick.

NOTES

[1]Ashley Montagu, *The Humanization of Man* (New York: Grove Press, Inc., 1962).

[2]*Time,* July 4, 1983, pp. 50,51.

[3]Gordon Wright, *In Quest of Healing* (Springfield, MO: Gospel Publishing House, 1984).

7

Dying, Death, and Grief

Precious in the sight of the Lord is the death of His saints (Psalm 116:15).

Should the subject of death be studied in school? Only a few years ago the idea sounded strange, and even objectionable. When death became a topic for discussion in public schools, many Christian parents protested strongly. They were opposed to any treatment of death and dying without mention of God or eternal life.

But today the subject is taught on almost every educational level, and, in some cases, it is taught in ways that encourage doubts concerning religious beliefs. College students study textbooks covering every aspect of the physical process of death, the experience of dying, elements and stages of grief, analyses of behavior at funerals, and counseling of the bereaved. Scholars have made use of the Greek word *thanatos,* the word for death in the New Testament, to name this new field of study *thanotology.*

Not only in school, but also in the popular literature there is an explosion of interest in death. One explanation for this is a general movement toward the examination and open discussion of every minute detail of human life and behavior. Also, this interest results from the science-fiction-like quality we see in modern medicine and technology.

Through dramatic, detailed media reports, we have experienced the plastic heart. We have heard pleas for live human organs for transplant into dying children, and have agonized with families trying to decide when to remove life support equipment from loved ones. We have watched the actual televised sessions where doctors vote on who will get a kidney machine and who will be left to die. We have heard heated arguments over the issues of life. *When does life begin and when does it end?* Today, even the most educated and sincerely concerned experts cannot agree upon a definition of death. At least one state (Kansas) has enacted a statute that establishes two alternative definitions of death. The question is raised: Does a living body turn into a corpse by biological means only, or by the signing of an official document?

That these matters affect Christian teaching was made plain in one Sunday school recently when a class broke up in anger and confusion over the subject of heart transplants. It is the duty of every Sunday school teacher to be as well-prepared as possible to manage discussions of this type. Definite answers may not be available, but the questions cannot be squelched.

If the subject of death and dying is not to be turned over completely to non-Christian treatment in school, then the church must assume responsibility. It is not a matter that can be handled by occasional preaching of a sermon, or by inviting professional psychologists to speak for annual seminars. The need is for consistent and competent education, keeping people informed and prepared to cope with basic issues and personal needs.

Dying and Death

Certainly the Bible is not silent on the subject of death. The first recorded conversation in the Garden of Eden refers to death (Genesis 2:17). Within four chapters there is murder, and by chapter seven, every creature outside the ark has known the agony of drowning. Biblical authors do not hesitate to show that death has always been an ugly, painful puzzle in human experience.

Young's Analytical Concordance to the Bible lists 350 references under the heading *death*, 135 references under *mourn-*

ing, and 97 under *grief* and *grieving.*[1] In the Old Testament very little comfort is given in any of the references to death. They are matter-of-fact statements. People just died or were killed and no elaboration is given. "Adam lived 930 years, and then he died" (Genesis 5:5). "Cain attacked his brother Abel and killed him" (Genesis 4:8). The first hint of heaven is found in the words, "he was gathered to his people" (Genesis 25:8).

However, we know that people feared death from the beginning, since even though he killed his brother, Cain begged not to be killed (Genesis 4:14). A detailed example of mourning is given in the death of Jacob (Genesis 49:29 to 50:10). The notion that grief should be "worked through" for a certain period of time is implicit in expressions such as, "The Israelites grieved for Moses . . . thirty days, until the time of weeping and mourning was over" (Deuteronomy 34:8).

The writer of Ecclesiastes gives voice to man's most pessimistic fears: old age is increasingly miserable and meaningless, and after death there is no hope (Ecclesiastes 9:4-10; 12:1-8). Here we get a glimpse of what the modern psychologists spend pages in declaring: *man's greatest need is for meaning. Meaning and hope are the only medicines that relieve the pain of dying and curb the inclination to suicide.*

In the Psalms and the prophetical books, we begin to sense that hope and meaning may be forthcoming. David's poetry includes pleas for protection from death, and he sees death as a dark valley in which evil may lurk. In his imagination death is likened to cords which entangle him, and the grave is anguish. Yet, he declares that there is comfort in the Lord, and that the death of His saints is precious in the sight of God. (Read Psalms 23, 116, and 118.) Throughout the Psalms there is an unmistakable note of victory over death in anticipation of the Saviour. Isaiah echoes for us the voice of God, saying, "My purpose will stand . . . . what I have planned, that will I do. . . . those who hope in Me will not be disappointed" (Isaiah 46:10,11; 49:23). Isaiah introduces the Messiah as a suffering servant, a man of sorrows, familiar with grief, who will through suffering bring salvation to mankind (Isaiah 53).

In the New Testament, hope and meaning are major themes. Words from the prophecies of Isaiah and Hosea are repeated with assurance. Death has been swallowed up in victory, and the grave has lost its sting! There is now specific promise of resurrection. We can rejoice and comfort one another with the knowledge that eternal life awaits all who believe in the Lord Jesus Christ (Isaiah 25:8; Hosea 13:14; 1 Corinthians 15; 1 Thessalonians 4:13-18).

In addition to Biblical knowledge, the preparation of the Sunday school teacher must include some knowledge of the current literature on dying and death. Some books written from the Christian viewpoint are available in bookstores, or by order from church publishers. General works may be found at the public library. It is important for the teacher to read this information to be familiar with the material students are exposed to in educational surroundings.

Among the most widely acclaimed publications is the book *On Death and Dying,* by Elisabeth Kubler-Ross.[2] This is the source of the outline on page 31 of the stages for facing crises. At this point we will examine briefly the work of Dr. Kubler-Ross as an example of how scholars view the subject of death and dying. Dr. Kubler-Ross is a psychiatrist who became aware that terminally ill patients seemed to go through a similar sequence of behaviors, or responses, to their condition. She decided to investigate this idea by giving patients opportunities to explain their own feelings and thoughts.

Dr. Kubler-Ross went about her project in a compassionate way, with a hospital chaplain as her colleague. They found that most of the patients realized the nature of their own condition, even though they had not been told. Terminal patients appreciated opportunities to express their true feelings freely, without the fear of hurting loved ones. The information from these interviews formed the basis for her work on the stages of dying, or coping with the dying experience.

The Christian teacher who has the wisdom, love, and patience to use some of these materials can learn how to meet the spiritual needs of dying persons and their families. The teacher, guided by the Holy Spirit, can use the Scriptures in helpful ways, and appropriate for the patients and their families the full resources of the Christian Body. Furthermore, what the teacher learns can be shared with the class, so that the members will know better how to minister to one another, and will be better prepared to cope with the crises that invade their own lives. It is with this purpose in mind that we consider the stages of coping with death.

Stages of Coping With Death

DENIAL

Patients who have a terminal illness go through a period when they deny they are sick. This step in coming to terms with the idea, or coping with the thought, is similar to denial of the aging process. Some people try to act cheerful, buy new clothes, take trips, or engage in extreme attempts to show death is not happening to them.

Some initial denial behavior is healthy, giving the individual time to develop ways of coping with a difficult situation. In our society, defiance of death is attributed to popular heroes in sports and fiction, so admission of illness may be considered weak and cowardly. Among Christians, admission of illness may be interpreted as lack of faith. Therefore, the individual must collect his thoughts and work out his own method of adjustment.

During the stage of denial there is frequently a cry for help. Doctors are implored to give assurance that there is hope. Christians may make frequent requests for prayer, and demand assurances from pastors and Christian friends of healing. Since the only true hope can come not from people but from God, these individuals need more than ever to be encouraged to read and meditate on the Scriptures. They need love and opportunities to share their feelings. The teacher should be a model of godly confidence, but should refrain from giving a quick assurance of healing just to make the sick person feel better momentarily. Class prayer meetings and prayer chains are more effective if they are an on-going part of the Body ministry, and not called upon just for emergencies.

ANGER

Anger is the usual reaction to frustration. When people who have had control of their bodies are confronted with mounting weakness and limitations, they feel that life is unfair and intolerable. So they are angry. This anger may be projected onto other people in what seems to be random and unreasonable ways. They may become envious of well people, and ask, "Why me?" Those who try to help them may become targets of accusations, complaints, and demands. This is a most difficult stage for everyone, since angry behavior causes angry responses. Those who do not understand the needs of the sick may take the outbursts of anger personally and scold or try to fight back. The anger subsides more quickly when it is allowed to run its course with as little reaction from others as possible. Usually a teacher should not try to reason with an angry person, nor shame him, even if he is angry with God.

BARGAINING

Dr. Kubler-Ross was impressed with the number of patients in her interviews who tried to make some kind of bargain for life, or just a little more time to live. Like Hezekiah (2 Kings 20:1-6), they asked for extensions on the basis of good behavior or worthwhile contributions to be made. Sometimes they asked only that death be delayed until they could accomplish a certain task or see a certain person. Sometimes the bargaining was a sign that the sick person felt guilty. This is one reason Dr. Kubler-Ross worked with a chaplain when she did the interviews. She felt the patient needed an opportunity to express guilty feelings and find relief so that more bargaining would not be necessary.

DEPRESSION

When a sick person can no longer deny illness, and the bargaining does not ward off the painful awareness of death, the result is overpowering feelings of loss and defeat. Two kinds of depression are described by Dr. Kubler-Ross. One is oriented to the present. There are worries over expenses, and what will become of children. Patients may feel they have failed to provide adequately or left an important task undone. At this point they may be encouraged by assurances concerning the welfare of their loved ones. Sometimes a frank discussion concerning the worrisome problems will help the person to feel more in control and his self-esteem will be supported.

The second type of depression is oriented toward the impending final loss of life on earth. At this time attempts at cheerfulness should be avoided. Friends should pray and give sincere expressions of appreciation for the patient as a person. The worst fate for a patient is to feel worthless and abandoned. Even Christ cried out against abandonment: "My God, my God, why have you forsaken me?" (Matthew 27:46).

ACCEPTANCE

In the typical sequence of steps there comes a time when the patient no longer feels angry or depressed. He simply accepts his coming end. This is not to be considered a hopeless resignation. The doctors say it is not a happy time, but a time almost void of feelings. For the Christian it may be different, as the thoughts of heaven change the situation in ways unbelievers cannot understand. Nevertheless, moments of silence may be the most meaningful communication to share. The dying one needs only reassurance that someone is near and cares.

At this point the family usually needs more help than the patient. When the patient is not elderly, there is a tendency for some family members, especially spouses and young children, to irrationally look upon death as a rejection of them. They may blame the loved one for leaving them, or God for depriving them of the loved one. When this happens, they need reassurance regarding the meaning of life and death. Christians may be able to minister to them now by simply reading the Bible and sharing their loss with them. The main point for teachers, however, is that such attitudes are much less likely to develop if these matters have been introduced beforehand, in regular class discussions, and if there has been consistently good teaching concerning the meanings of life and death.

The word *acceptance* has a unique meaning for Christians. This is one point at which the death studies in the textbooks are faulty. Some scholars say acceptance means the person is now willing to accept death as the final end. Christians accept death as an inevitable event because of the nature of the fallen world, but they accept, too, the promise that the dead in Christ will be raised incorruptible, and the mortal will take on immortality. Christians accept death as the gateway to life eternal. Psalm 116:15 expresses God's view of the Christian's death as "precious in the sight of the Lord." *The Living Bible* gives this Scripture extended meaning: "He does not lightly let them [saints] die." Testimonies from students who have experienced grief should be encouraged so that the subject of death will be perceived in the light of Christianity, not simply as a series of biological and psychological stages.

Grief and the Work of Grieving

Grief and mourning have always been with people, but these feelings have only recently been the subjects of methodological studies. People in various times and places have developed distinctive ways of coping with grief. Large public ceremonies, hired mourners, and elaborate processions of all kinds are done as expressions of the need to acknowledge the awful pain and loss caused by death. In our society, the tendency has been to try to keep grief more private and dignified. Some people feel the expression of grief is a weakness, or a lack of Christian faith. Modern psychologists (both non-Christian and Christian) tell us the expression of grief in a natural way is healthy and ought to be encouraged. It is, in fact, a kind of task to be worked through.

Stages of this "grief work" have been described in much the

same way as the stages of coping with death and other crises. First there is the shock of realizing that someone has died. If the death is sudden and tragic, it is a tremendous blow to the whole person. There is a pattern of physical sensations, such as dazed unreality, weakness, dryness of mouth, deep sighing, and sweating. Usually the first vocal response is one of denial. Most persons say something like, "Oh, no, it can't be!"

After the denial is over, there is a painful awareness stage. The dead person is almost constantly in mind. There is a struggle to free oneself from the strong attachment. There is a restlessness, searching, disorganization, and despair. Some people become hostile and angry. Some suffer guilt, and panic.

In the normal grief pattern, a stage of beginning recovery follows after about six months. The main characteristic of this stage is that people think they have recovered and then experience relapses of acute grief. Events, such as holidays, may bring back memories and the same grief returns. This happens less and less often for most people, and within a year they are able to establish new attachments and new ways of living.

The value of the idea of stages is that it helps us understand what is happening to people, and it gives us a tool to help them understand their own behavior. As people realize that grief is a normal process to be worked through they will not try to deny or hide it and cause themselves more problems. The "work" consists mostly in letting go of the past, proving to oneself that new meaning and purpose is possible, that life can be rebuilt. Obviously this process is not easy. It *is* work. If it is done consciously and well it can bring the reward of spiritual and personal growth—a new maturity. It is said that gain comes out of loss, because people who suffer grief recover with deeper appreciations, new capacities to love, and a clearer idea of what is important in life.

Abnormal Grief

Because of individual differences, some people may grieve much longer than others. For this reason it is difficult to say exactly when grief ceases to be normal. If any of the grief symptoms become extreme and persist for a long time, the grief may be pathological. Pathological grief is intense, prolonged, and prevents the person from resuming a normal life. The person may be unable to release himself from the dead person. He may experience feelings of helplessness, self-condemnation, and moodiness or withdrawal from reality. The teacher should be alert to people who are suffering abnormal grief and recommend special help.

As we consider the factors that influence the way people respond to death, we recognize once more how powerful Christian experience and education can be. Those who know what the Bible teaches about death and grief are much better equipped to handle their own sorrow. If they are surrounded by caring Christians who provide meaningful activity and prayer, they have another special advantage to help them through the work of grief.

Children and Death

One of the most effective ministries of the Sunday school teacher can be to help children learn about death, and provide knowledgeable and loving assistance to children and their families in times of bereavement.

The subject of death is not discussed in many homes because the parents do not know how to express constructive ideas on how to accept the death of a loved one. Most parents try to shield children from what they believe is unpleasant. They tell children that dead people are asleep or gone away. This often makes children afraid to go to sleep or take trips. A child thinks concretely, and he or she must be given information that may be simplified but absolutely truthful and reliable. Teachers of adults are responsible to help parents in this regard.

Teachers of parents of children, as well as teachers of children, should have some understanding of child development in order to help children learn about death at home as well as in Sunday school. The subject of death should be introduced without causing fear so the child will grow up with healthy attitudes.

Very young children can be taught the difference between life and non-life. People and pets and birds are alive and have feelings, but chairs are not alive. By the time the child is three, he can understand that live things die, such as birds or pets. Then he should be told about the death of people in plain, truthful terms. People die. God will take care of people who have died. That is enough until questions are asked. Even talk of heaven can have its complications. Children have tried to kill themselves in order to go to heaven and see mommy.

Very young children do grieve. Children have suffered brain damage and retarded physical growth from the shock of separation and loss when a parent dies. Older children may experience nightmares, eating problems, bed-wetting, nail-biting, and angry behavioral outbursts. Many children feel guilty, thinking they have caused the death by being bad. The reactions of most children result from their previous teaching, and what they see others do. When a parent dies and the surviving parent is suffering, the familiarity of the Sunday school surroundings and the presence of a trusted adult help to relieve the child's immediate pain. A wise and loving teacher can lay the foundation for healthy adjustments to death and other crises throughout life.

The grieving of adolescence is especially complex, since at this point the person is striving for independence and may have hostile feelings toward parents and siblings. If a parent or sibling dies, the adolescent may be thrown into great turmoil and guilt. The teacher of a bereaved teenager should indicate recognition and concern for the teenager as a person, not simply as a member of a saddened family. The pastor or a professional should be consulted if the student seems to have problems that are not being met.

Practical Suggestions for Teachers

When the subject of death arises, be open and honest. Encourage free discussion. Allow students to express their true feelings. Do not get impatient, shocked, or scold and contradict people who may express hostility, resentment, and anger.

Pray for the sick and bereaved during class time. Encourage an unhurried attitude of intercessory prayer. Be willing to help bereaved people make decisions if they ask. Help them to pray for guidance. Decisionmaking can be especially painful at this time.

Arrange for practical help for those with needs. Organize the class members to provide companionship, child care, transportation, household help, or whatever is appropriate.

Be especially sensitive in the handling of special days, since these are likely to bring memories and recurrence of grieving.

Remember that in times of serious sickness and bereavement people need to be treated as individuals—each in the way most appropriate for his own personality. Ask the Lord for guidance and help the class to be sensitive to these individual needs also. Usually just being with a sick or bereaved person, to listen and touch, is the best thing a Christian can do.

WHAT NOT TO SAY

Bereaved persons have reported that they prefer not to hear the following comments:
1. I know just how you feel.
2. It was God's will.
3. God needed him in heaven.
4. God wanted her to be with Him.
5. These things have a reason.
6. She is better off now.
7. God took him because he was so good.
8. She just went to sleep (or is just away).
9. You have other children, or you can have another child.

The following testimony relates how a teacher shared love in a time of death and grief.

My husband took the ringing phone quickly, trying not to

awaken me. But I heard him repeat in disbelief the devastating message. The parents of one of our Sunday school students had been in a horrible accident. The mother was dead, and the father seriously hurt.

We started praying and grabbing for our clothes. We team teach the young couples class and these students had become very close to us.

At the hospital we found this couple with other family members clinging to one another in painful shock. We joined them. That's all we could do. As we huddled together saying the name of Jesus over and over, hugging, crying, and experiencing this most awful grief, we were really thankful for the privilege of being there with them.

We were just there, offering our presence. But I think it was more than personal presence. We represented the love of all the class members. Our class is something special. We spend time in prayer for one another not only on Sunday; we meet for morning prayer meetings each week. We do fun things too, like a social time every month. On Valentine's Day we photograph each couple. We give them one copy, and put another copy on the classroom wall so we can remember the names and new couples can get acquainted.

Now in the time of crisis and sorrow, all this made new sense. We represented the trust and love accumulated from all the shared experiences. Christ in us reached out through our familiar beings to comfort them and reinforce their faith.

I opened my large purse and passed around the Kleenex. There was so much crying. How gratefully they took the tissues.

This is Body ministry, I thought with a new surge of wonder, as I wiped at my own streaming eyes. *Just to be here in this moment with exactly what they need—compassion, love, and Kleenex.*

Summary

Today there is an explosion of interest in the subject of death. The church must take its responsibility in teaching people to cope with personal grief, the process of dying, and death.

Modern psychologists agree that purpose—meaning—and hope are the only medicines that relieve the pain of dying. Christ provided both of these by His death and resurrection!

Dying persons and their families go through stages of coping with death. Dr. Kubler-Ross has defined these stages as denial, anger, bargaining, depression, and acceptance. Sunday school teachers must be aware of the emotions and reactions of people in these various stages so they can provide understanding and help.

NOTES

[1]Robert Young, *Young's Analytical Concordance to the Bible* (Grand Rapids, MI: Wm. B. Eerdmans, 1955).

[2]Elisabeth Kubler-Ross, *On Death and Dying* (New York: MacMillan Publishing Co., Inc., 1979).

8

Alcohol and Drug Abuse

*You were taught . . . to be made new in the attitude of
your minds. . . . Be very careful, then, how you live. . . .
Do not get drunk. . . . Instead be filled with the Spirit
(Ephesians 4:22,23; 5:15,18).*

Is It a Sin To Drink?

Sunday school students may bluntly ask if it is a sin to drink.
But they will not be satisfied with a blunt reply. The question
is complex, and teachers need to examine the subject of alcohol
and drug abuse in order to answer it properly.

Without doubt alcoholism and drug abuse are widespread
and very costly to individuals and to society. In addition to
health and family problems, they generate tremendous expense, involving, among other things, treatment, welfare payments, law enforcement, and destruction of property. In the
U.S., alcohol-related accidents kill 3 persons and injure 80 every
hour of every day—that's 25,000 deaths each year, to say nothing of the $24 billion burden left on society.

Alcoholism is called the great hidden health problem. Even
though much of its devastation is visible, much more of it is
not as apparent. One of every twenty North Americans will
become an alcoholic. Few people realize the effects of alcoholism
on children. Major birth defects are common in babies of drinking women. And alcoholism in either parent is a recognized
factor in cases of child abuse and neglect.

More than ever before, young people are abusing alcohol in
ways that disrupt their lives and threaten the health and safety

of themselves and others. Various studies have indicated that anywhere from 5 to 30 percent of high school students can be classified as problem drinkers.

The tremendous increase in marijuana production in this country and the cost to the public of trying to control the importation of drugs are reported almost every day in the newspapers. At least 45 million Americans have used marijuana, 10 million have taken cocaine, and about 650,000 are addicted to heroin.

Most use of illegal drugs begins before the age of 17, and the "drug problem" usually is perceived in terms of street gangs and rock parties. However, there is another drug problem, one of gigantic proportions. That is the abuse of over-the-counter and prescription products. An NBC news broadcast in June 1983 reported that the abuse of prescription drugs is extremely serious in nursing homes. The investigators quoted on the program had documented 30,000 deaths resulting from medications. One person in the study was using 22 different prescription drugs at the time of death.

Another source reports that in one year enough amphetamines and barbiturates are prescribed to provide every person in the United States with a month's supply. About one third of all people between 18 and 74 years of age have had prescriptions for some kind of tranquilizers and sleeping medicines. To this can be added untold amounts of pain relievers and other chemical substances obtained without prescriptions.

What does all this have to do with the question of sin? It helps us to consider our approach to the meaning of sin. We may be thinking of the behavior and not the cause of the behavior. We become aware that drinking socially, being an alcoholic, using drugs in youth gangs, and using excessive amounts of drugs in various medications must be linked in some way. We keep coming back to the question, "What needs are people trying to meet?"

One writer has suggested that the extremely serious nature of drug and alcohol abuse ought to present Americans with a moment of truth: Why is this happening? Is it just a wave of crime that should be stamped out by law enforcement? Is it simply caused by the heartless, greedy criminal element we see in television drama? Or is it possible to get rich pushing drugs because so many people have not found better ways to meet their needs? If young people cannot find a set of values to rely on and a place to belong and feel accepted, they will search for something to fill the emptiness. If the pain and loneliness of the elderly and others who feel left out in this impersonal society are not recognized and treated in better ways, some will turn to alcohol and other forms of legal and illegal drugs.

From this point of view, drinking and drug abuse are to a great extent *the result of some need or lack in the lives of people.* The Scriptures imply this, as we have seen in the quotation from Ephesians. We could paraphrase Ephesians 5:15-18 like this: "Don't get drunk to satisfy the needs of your life. That is the foolish and empty way of the world; it only leads to more trouble. The wise and happy way to find satisfaction is to be filled with the Holy Spirit."

We know the true meaning of life is found only in Christ. So our task as Christian educators is to help people learn this and prepare their minds and emotions to receive the guidance of the Spirit. To do this we need to understand more fully the problem of alcohol and drug abuse, to learn how to present Christ more effectively to those with drug and alcohol problems, and to learn how to help prevent others from seeking satisfaction in the wrong way.

What Is Meant by Substance Abuse?

The word *substance* is used to include both alcohol and drugs, legal and illegal, as well as anything (such as glue and nasal spray) that can be used in an excessive way to produce physical and emotional effects. Alcohol is a drug. Attitudes toward substances, and whether or not substances are legal, are based partly on social and cultural factors. Substances that are accepted in one culture may be rejected in another. In this country using a small amount of marijuana is illegal, but drinking a dangerous amount of alcohol is not. Whether society regards these substances as legal or illegal, both are potentially addictive drugs.

COMMONLY ABUSED DRUGS

Note: There are legitimate medical uses for some of the following drugs and any students who may be taking these under a doctor's care should not be put under condemnation.

Narcotics—induce sleep and relieve pain (opium, morphine, heroin, codeine)
Synthetic narcotics are Percodan, Dolophine, Demerol, Darvon.

Volatile Liquids—produce drowsiness, dizziness, hallucinations (benzine, carbon tetrachloride [glue sniffing])

Hypnotic-Sedatives—suppress the brain functions and cause sleep (barbiturates, such as Veronal and phenobarbital, alcohol, bromides, Placidyl, Valmid, Dalmane, Ditran, methyprylon)

Antihistamines—prevent the action of histamines in the body, can produce drowsiness and sleep

Tranquilizers—relieve tension (Valium, Equanil, Phobex, Librium, Librax)

Hallucinogens—create vivid distortions in the senses (LSD, mescaline)
Marijuana often is classified as a hallucinogen but may also be placed under other classifications.

Cocaine—produces violent stimulation and euphoria (known as "snow" or "coke")
It comes from the South American coca plant and is the most powerful natural stimulant known.

Antidepressants—affect the hormone levels in the brain causing the individual to feel alert, energetic, and happy; counteract drowsiness, inactivity, indifference, and general depression (Marplan, Niamid, Nordil, belladonna)

Amphetamines—stimulate the central nervous sytem

Diet pills are in this group (Benzedrine, Dexedrine); common names are Bennies, Dexies, Whites, Speed

Anesthetics—the most potent of the nervous system depressants (most often abused is PCP, known as "angel dust" or "peace pills"; it is extremely dangerous)

COMPARISON OF POTENTIAL FOR ADDICTION

Some drugs have higher potential for addiction than others. With high-potential drugs (such as heroin), usage will lead to addiction in a short time and the effects are very dangerous. Caffeine is a very mild drug. Addiction will take longer and usually the effects are not significant. The rest fall somewhere in between:

> Heroin
> Morphine
> Demerol
> Cocaine
> Barbiturates
> Amphetamines
> Alcohol
> Tranquilizers
> Codeine
> Bromides
> Nicotine
> Marijuana
> Caffeine

ALCOHOL

There are three common kinds of alcohol. Methyl alcohol (wood alcohol) is used in antifreeze and fuels. It is a deadly poison and very small amounts can cause blindness and death. Isopropyl alcohol is the principal ingredient of rubbing alcohol. It, too, is poisonous. The alcohol used for beverages is ethyl alcohol (also known as ethanol) and grain alcohol.

All alcoholic beverages contain ethyl alcohol, which is produced by fermentation of sugar. Consequently, their calorie count is high. But their food value is nil—no minerals, no usable nutrients (except an insignificant amount in beer).

All alcoholic beverages are mood-altering drugs that can seriously affect the normal functioning of the mind and the body. They all have the same general effects. The only difference among alcoholic drinks is the amount of alcohol they contain. Alcohol in beer and wine has the same effects as alcohol in whiskey.

Are There Physical Reasons for Substance Abuse?

Is there something about the body of one person that makes him more likely to become addicted to alcohol or other drugs? One theory proposes that innate defects, such as allergies, make addiction certain for some people if one drink is taken.

However, most of those who have studied this question see little evidence of a physical basis for addiction. The person who abuses drugs and alcohol *chooses* to do so. In most cases, the desire for a thrill, for a new experience, or for acceptance is the reason for first-time experiences. Whether the person goes on to become addicted depends not on his body type or hormones but on his emotional needs and circumstances.

Psychological Theories

Freudian psychologists, who attribute most human behavior to unconscious tendencies, believe alcoholism may reflect a subconscious death wish. The person is hostile toward himself and drinks for self-destruction. They also believe obsessive drinking can indicate latent homosexuality. Television commercials show men drinking together, having a good time, so friendly association with men is connected with heavy drinking.

Other theories involve conflicting desires for dependency or power. People feel they cannot be blamed for their behavior and should be excused from personal responsibility when they are under the influence of alcohol or other drugs. At the same time, if they have felt depressed, and worthless or rejected, the drugs make them feel more powerful.

The most useful psychological theories for Christian teachers are those concerning the basic needs. The universal search for meaning in life is an indication that we are created in the image of God. We have a natural longing to find our place in His great plan. This basic need is experienced by people as *needs for security, love, self-esteem,* and *creative expression.* Psychologists, who observe human behavior, are able to identify these needs. They say people are more likely to become dependent on drugs if they feel insecure, unloved, put down, or blocked from opportunities to develop and express their potential.

Social Theories

Sociologists emphasize the relationship of the individual to society, institutions, and other individuals. One theory is that when people experience the influence, pressure, or persuasion of society and its demands, they tend to adjust in three main ways: *conformity, rebellion,* and *retreat.*

Today may people fall into the traps of advertising campaigns and believe what they see on television is natural and must be copied if life is to be full and exciting. They begin to think it is masculine or sophisticated to use alcohol. They begin to think that every small pain and problem requires medication. Thus *conformity* can lead to substance abuse.

Another kind of conformity is to believe that one must do what everyone else does in order to be accepted into a group. Beginning to drink and experiment with drugs is almost always a social experience for the young. Substance abuse results more frequently from peer pressure than from any other cause.

Sometimes conformity to the behavior of one group is related to *rebellion* against another. For example, teenagers who are trying to express rebellion against the restrictions of the home may be drawn into conformity with a peer group. The so-called drug subculture is an expression of rebellion against the accepted values of the society. The recent increase in alcoholism among women has resulted partly from the efforts of women to conform to the popular image of the liberated person and to rebel against the traditional role of women.

For other people, substance abuse becomes a way of *retreat.* Many lonely housewives do not rebel, but rather withdraw into secret drinking or become addicted to Valium, as was the case with Betty Ford. People who lose their jobs, get divorced, or in other ways feel embarrassed, ashamed, rejected, or guilty, may drink as a means of retreat. They do not want to face people, or they think they cannot meet the expectations of society.

Typical Steps to Dependency and Addiction

How do people become dependent on alcohol and other drugs? What path do they follow to become addicted? Although every case has unique features, some patterns are common.

Most teenagers start drinking beer or smoking marijuana or tobacco as a matter of curiosity. "Everybody" is doing it and experimenting seems harmless. Most young people who come from close, loving families where they have been taught Christian principles and the dangers of drugs experience no great temptation to go further. But if the young person is rebelling against the family, if he feels rejected or too restrained, if his home is broken by divorce, then the independence of the peer group and the physical sensations induced by the drugs may seem attractive, and the way is paved for more and more indulgence. After a time the person finds that when he or she is deprived of the substance, discomfort results. This may be anything from a craving to an actual withdrawal experience. *Withdrawal* is the painful physical illness that results from being deprived of drugs after the person has become addicted. Some people do not realize they are addicted until they try to stop taking the substance.

For most adults alcoholism develops gradually from social drinking, or from the practice of having a drink to ease tension at the end of the day. If tension mounts and life becomes too stressful, or if life seems meaningless and boring, the tendency is to drink more and more until alcoholism results. Wilbur Mills, a congressman who had to leave office because of alcoholism, now gives lectures to try to help others. He describes his experience in this way. If he had not been drinking, he would have sought other means of improving his life. But *since he had already started drinking,* when his problems became too much for him, he simply drank more. He went from one drink before dinner to two quarts of vodka a day. He declares that alcoholism is a disease and that anyone with a drinking problem must seek help, because alcoholics cannot help themselves.

The other typical path to substance abuse for persons of all ages is inability to cope with crisis. Loss, disappointment, feelings of being rejected, loneliness, failure to meet expectations of self or others may lead to physical or emotional symptoms, for which the person may seek prescriptions from a physician. These symptoms include headaches, nervousness, and sleeplessness. If the person facing a crisis comes from a background where alcohol was used, the tendency is to drink. If the person belongs to a social group where drugs are used and available, the tendency is to use drugs as a way of escape. When a problem arises, people try to cope in ways that are related to their teaching and background.

What Is Being Done About Substance Abuse?

The major issue in discussions of treatment for substance abuse is this: Is addiction a crime to be treated with law enforcement and punishment or is it a medical problem to be treated as a disease? The modern trend is to call it a disease, and to point out that the prohibition law was a failure and punishment does not bring results.

On the other hand, the disease concept has some major flaws. It implies that some people are unable to take a drink without overdoing it. But this disease does not compel anyone to become its victim—to take the first few drinks.

Today programs for control of substance abuse and rehabilitation centers are numerous. (Coupled with that, the prosecution of drunk drivers is becoming more effective.) The most successful program, according to most experts, is Alcoholics Anonymous. Christian educators should note that the system used by AA emphasizes education and group support, and has strong religious overtones. The alcoholic must express a sincere desire to stop drinking and acknowledge his helplessness. He must be sorry for his past failures and put forth real effort to overcome the habit. He must accept help and try to help others as well.

For young people, the Teen Challenge program has brought new life and hope to many who were addicted to alcohol and other drugs. A Christian ministry, it offers not only group work and counseling, but also residential facilities and adequate supervision. The program offers many opportunities for interacting with peers, witnessing, and living out the faith.

All drug rehabilitation efforts emphasize the importance of the family. Families have been known to hinder rehabilitation in two ways: Some families reject the abuser, others help him hide the problem.

What Can the Christian Teacher Do?

ATTITUDE AND BEHAVIOR OF THE TEACHER

Teachers must examine their own hearts and develop attitudes that will make them effective helpers. They must find the balance of accepting people without excusing them for weaknesses that can be overcome with God's help. They should recognize that alcoholism is not a disease in the same way as cancer or diabetes. On the other hand, it cannot be cured by punishment, scolding, and preaching.

Teachers must examine their own behavior and be sure they are not overly dependent on chemical substances of any kind. They should seek the Lord for victory over any tendency to use medications for every pain and sleepless night or every feeling of tension and stress. An overcoming model who faces life realistically and cheerfully is the best friend a substance abuser can have.

BACKGROUND FOR UNDERSTANDING

Teachers should read books and periodicals that give reliable information on substance abuse, including its prevention and treatment. They should visit local meetings of Alcoholics Anonymous when they have open sessions, and a treatment center or halfway house if one is in the community. Sometimes local hospitals or civic organizations sponsor seminars or special meetings designed for public information. Members of the class should be encouraged to attend also. Sometimes those who have overcome problems are willing to share their experiences if teachers show interest in them and give them appropriate opportunities.

USE OF THE BIBLE

Teachers have the obligation to understand what the Bible says and implies about substance abuse. To say simply that Christians shouldn't drink is inadequate. To build credibility with young people and to be good scholars (see 2 Timothy 2:15), teachers should know and teach exactly what the Bible teaches.

The use of wine is the only related topic mentioned specifically in the Word. Some references show that wine was considered to have healing properties. Jesus drank wine, and the drinking of wine is mentioned a number of times with no note of condemnation.

On the other hand, abstinence from wine is commended, as in the case of John the Baptist and the Nazarites. Many explicit warnings are given throughout the Old and New Testaments concerning overindulgence in wine. It is recognized as a very real danger to one's service of the Lord.

Biblical principles justify the teaching of abstinence, especially in modern society where the dangers of substance abuse are so great and the results so destructive. A good summary of relevant Biblical principles is given by Gary Collins, some of which follow:

Christians are not to break the law, so anything illegal or unethical is to be avoided (Romans 13:1-5; 1 Peter 2:13-17).

Christians are not to allow themselves to be controlled by anything (1 Corinthians 6:12).

Burdens are to be taken to the Lord. We are not to try to cover them or escape in some artificial way, such as by taking drugs (1 Peter 5:7; Psalm 55:22).

We are to use the good things God has given us for good purposes, and the use of His creation for questionable and destructive practices is to be avoided (Genesis 1:28).

God absolutely condemns drunkenness, which certainly includes control of the person by any chemical substance (Proverbs 20:1; 23:29-31; Isaiah 5:11; Romans 13:13; 1 Corinthians 5:11; 6:10; Galatians 5:21; Ephesisns 5:18; 1 Thessalonians 5:7,8; 1 Peter 4:3).

The body is to be kept pure, since it is the dwelling of the Holy Spirit (1 Corinthians 6:19,20; Romans 12:1). Escaping through chemical means is the world's phony substitute for the infilling of the Holy Spirit (Ephesians 5:18).[1]

CLASS PRESENTATIONS AND ACTIVITIES

Teachers of Children

Do not be afraid to use basic facts. Children see drinking and drugs on television. Some drinking and drug problems occur as early as elementary school, so children should be given opportunities to ask questions and receive competent answers in Sunday school. Look in the public library for children's books on drugs and drinking. Be sensitive to the needs of children who may be exposed to alcoholism at home. Local mental health centers may have some literature to help with this situation. Alcoholics Anonymous has a branch program for families of alcoholics.

Teachers of Young People

Young people respect adults who are aware of the real world and its problems. Be open and honest with them. Let them know you are concerned about their need to be accepted by their peer group. Discuss ways of overcoming pressure. Arrange a class visit to a drug abuse center. Invite social workers and young people with victorious testimonies to share with the class. Be sensitive to the needs of individuals; see that no one is left out or neglected. Watch for signs of personal distress, depression, or hostility. Offer opportunities for personal confidences without threat of recrimination or disclosure, and suggest sources of help when needed. In class pray specifically for the students to receive guidance and strength as they face the problems and temptations of the week. Let them leave the class with a sense of your concern and support.

Teachers of Adults

If you can help adults find meaning and purpose in life and hope for the future, you will be providing the best possible prevention and treatment. Emphasize to parents the extreme importance of their example, and of honest communication and happy family relations. For those who are worried about their adolescent children, you can help them understand the needs and problems of teenagers. You can organize special prayer meetings for parents to pray for their children. You can help them select books and work with parents to provide the guidance their children need.

Summary

1. Substance abuse most often becomes a problem for people whose deepest needs have not been met, for those who have not learned to cope with crisis events.

2. People who have a genuine experience with Christ and are taught from the Bible find true values, meaning, and satisfaction; they are not likely to be attracted to alcohol and

drugs, even though they may experiment as a result of curiosity and peer pressure.

3. Happy relationships with people help individuals develop feelings of self-worth and the ability to cope with life.

4. Early, honest teaching helps people understand the dangers of drugs and resist group pressure.

NOTES

[1]Gary R. Collins, *Christian Counseling* (Waco, TX: Word Books, 1980).

9

Work, Unemployment, and Money

*Keep your lives free from the love of money and be content
with what you have, because God has said, "Never will I
leave you; never will I forsake you" (Hebrews 13:5).*

"Who is she?"

"Well, I think she's a teacher at Central Junior High."

"Good morning, sir. I'm glad to have you in the class today.
I don't believe I've seen you here before."

"No. I work at the X Company. One of our salesmen attends
this church and invited me to come."

These are typical bits of conversation that illustrate the tendency people have to be connected to their work. This association is not new. God connected himself with work when He
completed creating the world. "On the seventh day he rested
from all his work" (Genesis 2:2). Man was first connected with
work in the Garden. "There was no man to work the ground"
(Genesis 2:5) until God told Adam and Eve to take care of His
garden.

We notice man's association with work throughout the Scriptures. Amos was a shepherd who also took care of sycamore-
fig trees; Peter and Andrew were fishermen; Matthew was a
tax collector; Jesus was called the carpenter's son; Lydia was
a dealer in purple cloth; Paul, Aquila, and Priscilla were tentmakers. Many unnamed Bible characters are designated by
occupation: the centurion, the ruler. And most of the parables

involve working: farming, making bread, hiring workers, sweeping the house.

It seems logical that a working, creating God would build into His people the need and desire to be active and to utilize their energies and abilities. Work itself was a gift. The curse came with the Fall, when work became a difficult chore, as well as a necessity for survival. Even then God left it in man's nature to get satisfaction from work.

Christianity brings a renewed meaning to work, as it does to all human experience. Work is now to be done not only as a beneficial activity necessary to survive, but also as a means to have something to share with those in need (see Ephesians 4:28). How beautiful, consistent, and comprehensive is the plan of God!

Since the need to make a living is so much a part of being human, it follows that many of man's troubles and problems will involve employment and money. In times of economic instability especially, almost every other difficulty is complicated by financial matters. Most obvious is the problem of unemployment. Someone in the Sunday school class may say, "Pray that the Lord will help me find a job." The prayer is made, and everything goes on as usual, in most cases. Behind that simple request, however, may be problems of major proportions. Sensitive teachers will want background knowledge so they can understand such problems and use the teaching ministry to help class members solve them.

Unemployment—The Emotional Impact

Today when we speak of unemployment and say people need jobs, we usually are thinking in terms of the need for money to buy food and pay rent. Actually a job is much more. It is an indication of personal worth. It is something specific to do with one's time. It is an indication of one's social status. It is a way to have a social life, or at least relationships with people. People who lose jobs lose self-esteem, friends, meaningful activity, a way of describing themselves to others, and the satisfaction of feeling they have some control over their lives. Unemployed people may feel that life has lost its meaning, that they have failed their families, that they have been cheated and abused, or even that God has failed them.

To understand the importance of work and the intense suffering of many unemployed people, it is necessary to examine history. People once understood the purpose of work not as making money but as producing something useful. A craftsman produced one item from start to finish. He had the satisfaction of seeing the results of his own labor. Other people could see the product and give credit to the artisan. The artisan felt that he had achieved something and that he was recognized for his work. These are two basic needs of human beings: achievement and recognition.

Today we seldom connect a product with the workman. We have no way of knowing whether a certain person is good at his work or not. The result is that people are not judged according to what they produce or the quality of their workmanship. Rather they are judged by the title of their position and the amount of money they get. It is assumed that the occupational label is a measurement of every other quality of a person. If a person has a "good job" (which usually means a good salary), then we tend to consider him intelligent, efficient, capable, successful, and worthy of respect and certain privileges.

Usually people with good jobs judge themselves in much the same way as they are judged by others. In most cases they cannot have the satisfaction of producing a completed product. They do one operation in a long process in manufacturing, sales, or professional or semiprofessional services. The only meaningful measurement of their worth is the amount they are paid.

Even wealthy people who do not need money express great satisfaction at being paid high wages because this proves to them that they are worthy. Sometimes the most effective and successful homemakers, who in rearing human beings do the greatest work there is, feel put down because they are not on a salary! So achievement and recognition are put into terms of

"good jobs." People who have had good jobs and become unemployed may not have any other measurement of self-worth.
Consequently they feel like failures.

Another point of history helps explain the emotional effects
of unemployment: the work ethic. During early Christian times
people thought in terms of a secular-sacred division of activities, particularly between secular and religious vocations. This
led to an extreme separation between those who devoted their
lives to religious matters and those who gave themselves to
"ordinary" tasks, in other words, the lay people. The Protestant
Reformation broke down this wall so that all believers could
have the Scriptures and think of themselves as having a mem-
bership in the Kingdom equal with the religious leadership. A
further elevation of the laity occurred through the Calvinist
teaching that any kind of work ought to be done as unto the
Lord, and diligence in any occupation was a virtue. In America
this doctrine was developed to the point that Christianity and
hard work were almost inseparable. A good Christian man was
obligated to provide well for his family. Many people tried to
prove by hard work and economic success that they had God's
approval on their lives.

Although our country may not now hold this view of work,
it remains in our history, and perhaps our subconscious. Thus
it may explain why some people take the extreme position that
almost any unemployment represents a personal fault. The
feeling persists that something must be wrong with a person
who cannot make money. Even when it has been shown that
economic conditions make it impossible for everyone to be employed, many believe most unemployed people lack ambition
or intelligence, or they are not living in God's will.

When people accept help, such as food stamps, they may be
looked upon as lazy. Many extravagances of the wealthy are
excused, but if a loving, unemployed father sacrificially saves
on food stamp purchases to afford one roast beef dinner for his
family, someone who sees him make that purchase is likely to
pass judgment, thinking of him as undeserving. This is an
illustration of the feeling that people with money and jobs are

more "deserving" or somehow better than people without money and jobs. It is no wonder the unemployed have emotional problems. They have lost not only jobs, but also their value as persons. Even if they are in our churches and we do not feel this way about them, the attitude is expressed often enough that they feel it inside, and they begin to judge themselves.

One unemployed person put it like this: "When you lose your job it strips you of everything that's supposed to hold you together. Whatever is power to you, or responsibility, whatever means freedom and choice, is gone. I had to ask myself, 'Who am I now? What will I do now?' "

We see, then, that many unemployed people have the same emotional tendencies as those we have studied in relation to other crisis situations. This event, which on the surface is a financial problem, may bring to light deep personal problems of the individual. In some cases the need for worth and self-esteem is more intense than the actual need for money. We see this in the fact that depression, family conflicts, child abuse, spouse abuse, abuse of tranquilizers and other drugs, drinking, and even suicide result from the crisis of unemployment.

Part of the problem, as in the case of illness, is a condition of living in a fallen world. People become victims of circumstances over which they have no control, and little can be done to change the basic situation. But certain aspects of most problems are caused by human attitudes and behavior. In the case of the unemployed, some individuals may suffer more than is necessary because of social stigma. But they may also suffer because of their own pride, jealousy, resentment, and misplaced values.

What Can a Christian Teacher Do?

SET THE EXAMPLE IN ATTITUDES AND ACTIONS

As we have learned, in any time of crisis, people need first of all to feel someone understands and cares. They do not need condemnation and judgment. This is why we have emphasized background knowledge. The more a teacher understands a problem or condition, the better able he will be to handle it in the right way, giving help and applying the Scriptures appropriately, without ignoring the problem or judging the individual. The teacher's example is always part of the lesson.

Unemployment should be acknowledged and discussed in class, but teachers should guide the class away from discussions of welfare cheating, use of food stamps, and other subjects that could bring more embarrassment than help. In language and behavior, the teacher should uphold the principle of the equality of individuals before God. The teacher should express personal concern and show genuine respect for individuals who face their problems with faith and courage. It should be evident that the teacher puts value on personal qualities, and not on social position.

TEACH BIBLICAL PRINCIPLES

God's Provision

People who are unemployed, those who have chronic financial problems, and those who are constantly worried about the future need to be assured of *God's provision* and learn to trust Him for their needs. Difficult times may come, even to Christians, but God has promised, "Never will I leave you; never will I forsake you" (Hebrews 13:5). "God will meet all your needs according to His glorious riches in Christ Jesus" (Philippians 4:19).

Teachers can help students see how different God's values are from the world's values. From the viewpoint of sociology there is *real* poverty and *relative* poverty. Individuals and families who suffer real poverty lack adequate food, shelter, clothing, education, and medical help. It is the responsibility of the church to do everything possible to meet these needs. In both the Old and New Testaments great emphasis is placed on the obligation of God's people to care for the poor.

In the United States, probably more suffering is caused by relative poverty. People feel deprived because they cannot have what they see others have and what advertising campaigns lead them to believe is necessary for happiness. In addition, relative poverty causes people to feel personally inadequate and guilty because they cannot provide certain comforts and pleasures for their families.

The pain of both real and relative poverty can be relieved through effective teaching of Biblical principles. Christ tells us not to worry and fret about material things, but to trust in our wise and caring God, who has demonstrated His love for us in all nature. "The pagans run after all these things," says Jesus. "Your heavenly Father knows that you need them. But seek first his kingdom and his righteousness, and all these things will be given to you as well" (Matthew 6:32,33). Many financial problems that break up families and cause untold distress could be solved simply by believing God knows more about what we really need than do the merchants who advertise on television.

The Danger of Materialism

The promise of God's provision is a comfort, but a warning comes with it—a warning against the danger of materialism. Throughout the Bible God pleads with people, through prophets and poets, through Jesus and the apostles. He begs and warns us not to be greedy, not to be foolish, and not to set up a false system of values.

> People who want to get rich fall into temptation and a trap and into many foolish and harmful desires that plunge men into ruin and destruction. For the love of money is a root of all kinds of evil. Some people, eager for money, have wandered from the faith and pierced themselves with many griefs (1 Timothy 6:9,10).

God expects people to earn enough to meet their needs and in many cases even allows them surplus. But loving money or thinking of material goods as more important than spiritual values is wrong. And believing that material goods will bring enduring happiness and satisfaction is foolish. "Whoever loves money never has money enough; whoever loves wealth is never satisfied with his income" (Ecclesiastes 5:10).

Right Ways To Handle Money

Teachers should share with their students some practical Biblical teachings regarding money. Gary Collins lists four major points.[1]

1. *Money should be gained honestly.* "He who has been stealing must steal no longer, but must work, doing something useful with his own hands" (Ephesians 4:28; see also Proverbs 10:9; 11:1).

2. *Money should be invested carefully.* (See Matthew 25:14-30; Luke 12:16-21.)

3. *Money should be spent realistically,* without getting into trouble over credit and debts. (See Proverbs 22:7; Matthew 18:23-35.)

4. *Money should be shared joyfully.* "God loves a cheerful giver" (2 Corinthians 9:6-11). Generosity and cheerful giving are themes found throughout the Bible. Paying tithes, giving offerings, and sharing with those in need are requirements for all who are dedicated to Christ.

Right Attitudes Toward Work

The fact that Christians are to have compassion for the poor, provide for their needs, and accept them without discrimination does not mean laziness or sloppy attitudes toward work are to be condoned. The Bible teaches that people should make every effort to support themselves (see 2 Thessalonians 3:7-12). Workers are exhorted to do their best, serve with honesty and goodwill, and be respectful of their employers.

Some people are continually unhappy and dissatisfied in their work, or think of it only in terms of money. True professionals and those who have a sincere interest in what they do usually do not complain about wages unless they are grossly underpaid. But to people who see little or no meaning in their work, the pay is a major concern. Missionaries and other gospel workers have been satisfied to work under actual poverty conditions and consider it a privilege, while some people who have many luxuries are resentful if another is paid more than they are.

Athletes and entertainers may believe that $100,000 a year is too little, because they measure their value as persons in terms of money.

A Christian will think of his work first in terms of opportunities to serve the Lord. If it is in teaching, nursing, or any of the helping professions, the welfare of the students and clients must be put before all else. If it is working with people in any way, the example and witness of the Christian must come before thoughts of personal gain. Whatever kind of work it is, it should be considered an opportunity to earn money in order to have something to share with others. People spend years in education preparing for work. Then they spend a large proportion of their time, energy, and creative talents in their work. To suppose that this large part of the total person can be left out in the consideration of the Christian life is inconceivable. Yet, one of the greatest areas of neglect in the church is that of teaching people how to relate to their work situation. Whatever the Sunday school teacher can do to fill this gap is of utmost importance to the development of the body of Christ.

Women and Work

God appointed both Adam and Eve the privilege and duty of taking care of His garden. He called Eve a *helper,* which could be taken as a designation of a working partnership, in cooperation with Adam in whatever occupation the two of them should engage in as "one flesh" (see Genesis 2:20-24). In the Bible, a woman's place as wife and mother did not keep her from many other kinds of work. The noble wife of Proverbs 21 is a classic example of this truth. And remember that Aquila and Priscilla were together called tentmakers, and Lydia dealt in purple cloth.

Today women have educational opportunities equal to those of men, and every day the number of career options is greater. Most young women feel challenged and eager to prove their abilities and have new work experiences. However, they feel diasppointed when Christian leaders do not seem to recognize their need to be individuals and rejoice with them. They want to be accepted as contributors in church matters and be invited to exercise their spiritual gifts.

If women become impatient and feel the church is indifferent to their abilities, they may fall prey to the philosophy in current publications that places the highest values on assertiveness and self-sufficiency, suggesting that interdependence with others is a weakness. These periodicals declare that to place the desires or feelings of anyone else above oneself is to be a doormat. For example, the popular feminist leader Linda Gordon says, "No woman should have to deny herself any opportunity because of her special responsibilities to her children . . . children are cared for at the expense of women's lives."[2] Such writings as these, available at every magazine counter, openly advocate leaving husbands and children if this is necessary to be an authentic and fulfilled person. Usually this fulfillment is in terms of a paid occupation.

Sunday school teachers must recognize the needs of these young women and the situation in which they find themselves. Most are willing to be guided by Biblical principles if these are competently taught by a person who is open and understanding. What a tremendous ministry it is for a mature Christian teacher to be able to help young women find ways of satisfying their needs for achievement and recognition, using their careers as instruments for Christian living and service! What a joy it is to help them find their places of service, allowing them to minister with their gifts and talents as the Lord leads.

At the same time, we must point out the clear indication in the Bible that no occupation on earth is more important than that of giving a human being the right start in life by providing love, care, and teaching in the home during early childhood. We must emphasize that the greatest injustice done to women in our time is not keeping them out of so-called male jobs, but rather failing to give them proper credit for bearing more than their share of responsibility in the most important job of all.

Sunday school teachers find in their classes several other types of working women to whom they must minister. As we

have noted in the chapter on single parents, some women struggle with the almost impossible tasks of trying to work and also
be both mother and father. These women are likely to have
critical financial needs. They may be justifiably upset because
of discrimination on the job. They need compassion, prayer,
support, and guidance in making scriptural applications that
will comfort and sustain them. Teachers, because they may
know the women's circumstances better than others in the
church, may be able to arrange for practical assistance when
it is appropriate.

Another group of women with special needs are those who
return to work because of financial emergencies in the home,
a sick husband or prolonged medical expenses for a child, for
example. Some women are trying to help their children or their
husbands through college. Some may be newly widowed or
divorced. Many of these women find their experiences traumatic and even frightening or frustrating. Usually, just the
teacher's awareness of the situation and concern for them is a
comfort. Often it is helpful to be able to discuss the experiences,
exchange ideas with other members of the class, and pray for
one another.

Other women, at the ages of about 35-50, are experiencing
the "empty nest" syndrome: Their children have left home.
These women may have no financial need but they do have the
need of something new and stimulating. They have education,
experience, abilities, and gifts. Their physical and mental health
require use of their energies. Often the church is weak here
and does not recognize this tremendous human resource. The
materialistic society therefore wins again because these women
feel they are worth more and can be more fulfilled by finding
jobs that pay money. Sometimes the Sunday school is almost
dying for lack of able workers, while these women with fine
abilities are typing reports or punching computer keys for some
organization whose purpose they do not even know. The Teacher
in Ecclesiastes would say, "Meaningless! Meaningless!" Dedicated Sunday school teachers can help to recruit these talented

women for meaningful positions in the church and show them how to find satisfaction in the service of the Lord.

Summary

Work means more to the individual than just a source of income. It is an indication of identity, self-esteem, social status; it provides relationships, meaningful activity, and gives the feeling of some control over life situations. Therefore when people lose their jobs, they need more than financial assistance.

The Sunday school class should be the place where unemployment is acknowledged and discussed, where the Body responds with concern and understanding. Emphasize God's promise of provision and show genuine respect for personal qualities, not social position. In the giving to meet needs, do not take away the dignity of the people in need. Finally, material need and how we acquire it must be considered in light of eternal values (see Matthew 6:33).

NOTES

[1]Gary R. Collins, *Christian Counseling* (Waco, TX: Word Books, 1980).

[2]Linda Gordon, "The Nuclear Family: A Source of Neurotic Dependency," *Social Problems—The Contemporary Debates,* John B. Williamson, et al., eds. (Boston: Little, Brown and Co., 1981).

10

Identity Crisis

I praise you because I am fearfully and wonderfully made (Psalm 139:14).

"Be yourself." That is a bit of advice almost everyone has heard. Almost every parent and teacher has said it some time to a person facing a new or overwhelming experience.

"How shall I act?" they are asked. "What shall I do? I'll never be able to do it like—"

"Just be yourself."

Then other questions begin to form. "But what is being myself? Who am I, really? How do I know when I am being true to myself?"

In this way, most of us have become conscious of the concepts of self and personal identity. What most people do not realize is that these concepts are involved in much of the heartache and confusion in our lives. Feelings of guilt, inferiority, resentment, and blame are related to how we feel about ourselves. The ability to relate in positive ways with other people is also affected by what we believe about ourselves. How we develop as mature, productive Christians depends to some extent on the way we answer the question, "Who am I?"

Although most people have heard the expression *identity crisis,* and many use it frequently, few know exactly what it means. In fact, the concept of *identity* is not really understood by those who say, "I want to find myself. I want to find my identity." The self and identity are not something that can be "found." *Identity is a set of relationships and meanings.* A

128

person cannot find a ready-made identity, but must choose and develop his identity little by little from his life experiences.

Identity Crisis and the Life Span

Identity is formed from interaction between the individual and other people, and the adaptations a person makes to the changing situations of life. An identity *crisis* is an event in which some of the relationships are changed, and new adaptations must be made.

The term identity crisis came first out of Erik Erikson's studies of adolescence. Erikson states that the basic identity crisis is the need of the adolescent to pull away from parental values and develop personal values.[1] The young person feels a need for establishing a new kind of relationship with his parents, as an adult rather than a child. At this point in life the person begins to learn that every individual needs to be both dependent and independent. Until this truth is accepted by adolescents, parents, and everyone, confusion and unhappiness will result.

Today it is popular to talk about finding one's identity and living up to one's potential as though there were one *identity package* and one *potential package* for each individual. In reality, each person becomes identified, not in an empty space that contains only himself, but when he commits himself to something or someone with which to be identified. As we have seen in the Scripture passages, being a special person in the sight of God identifies us immediately with the Lord, His people, and His work. As for potential, Socrates said long ago that each person has the potential to do and become any number of things. Of course no one ever becomes everything he is capable of becoming, and certainly no one wishes to. The point is, we must choose which potential we want to live up to. We must select something beyond and greater than ourselves that is to become part of the real us.

Bible teachers can point out, to both adults and teenagers, that the need to pull away and establish identity is illustrated in the life of Jesus. The account of the trip to the temple shows a typical teenager at the task of formulating his own person, and a typical mother being concerned and unhappy about her child's independent behavior. Of course Jesus went back home with His earthly parents and was obedient to them. Later, His life indicates that even though He instituted some radically new ideas and ways of behavior, He never rejected His earthly parents or the religious principles they had taught Him in childhood.

Usually adolescents discover they do not need to find brand-new values in order to be detached in healthy ways from their parents, and they do not need to reject their parents as persons, to whom respect is due. They do, however, need to make their own decisions about accepting parental values and relationships as part of their own special identity. This is what we mean by choosing one's identity. The new kinds of relationships and the new personal meanings placed on the values and ideas—these help to form the new identity.

We know that identity as a Christian involves making a decision about a personal relationship with Christ. In a similar manner, all aspects of identity formation require the making of decisions and the forming of relationships. The search for identity is a search for somebody and something to identify with, to make a commitment to. There is no mysterious, hidden, authentic self to be discovered.

These truths, which should be learned as one passes through the identity crisis of youth, can be applied in other types of identity crises throughout the life span. One of these, which we discussed earlier, is the mid-life crisis. It is basically an identity crisis in which relationships and meanings change and the individual must find satisfactory adaptations. As children leave the home, a change takes place in their relationship with their parents, and this affects the relationship *between* the parents. Their priorities about how time and money are to be used may change. The relationship of the wife to the school, community, and church change. There may be time for outside work, new social contacts, service projects, the exercise of gifts and abilities that were put aside while the children grew. The husband may find the meaning of his work has changed for him. He feels displaced by younger people and new technologies.

Recently in our society it has become quite common and acceptable for people at this point in life to say, "I have given my life for my family all these years. Now I will do something for *me*." They may go off, much as adolescents, looking for identity, even thinking they must reject their marriage. The truth, for most of them, is that some goals have been attained. Rather than not having fulfillment, they have fulfilled certain potentials and now have opportunities to adapt their energies to new interests, to discover and fulfill other potentials.

Alert Sunday school teachers can help mid-life couples understand this, and then perhaps assist them in finding positions of service that are gratifying for both husband and wife, and also of inestimable value to the church program. For example, mature Christian couples are very successful as team teachers for young married couples. They can open their homes for midweek Bible study and social times, as well as teach the Bible on Sundays from husband and wife viewpoints. Some churches have husband-and-wife teams direct a senior citizens program, meeting on a Saturday for a morning session and then lunch. Connected with this, or as a separate project, outreach services for the elderly or shut-in can be offered.

Music is another area of service where people can serve as couples. In some churches a couple is given responsibility for the planning and arrangements (decorations, tickets, etc.) for the Christmas program. Other couples find pleasant activities to share, for example, singing in the choir or playing in the orchestra. Some are put in charge of missionary conventions and church outings. Couples who have sufficient financial resources can spend their summers with missionary construction teams who build churches and schools in foreign and home missions projects. For early retirees, short missionary assignments are available (e.g., through MAPS) where builders, printers, bookkeepers, and various other skilled workers can serve.

No other agency is better equipped than the church for providing adults with meaningful activities they can share in an environment where they will be supported and their contributions appreciated. And no other kind of situation has a better potential for giving assistance to those with identity problems.

Identity and Other Changing Relationships

A common type of identity crisis is experienced in the stepfamily. For example, suppose a teenage girl has been "lady of the house" since the death or divorce of her mother. Then her father remarries, and she is displaced. An important function and meaning has been taken from her: who she was in relation to her father. She may react in resentment and hostility, or in depression, withdrawal, and feelings of worthlessness. Her emotions may be interpreted as hate for the stepmother; in reality they may represent distress at her own loss of identity.

Identity crisis can also occur from a change in relationship brought about when elderly parents must be cared for. If they are brought to live with a younger family, everyone may experience problems. The older couple is used to being in control and may feel worthless and dependent. Or the younger wife may feel displaced by the mother or mother-in-law to whom she feels she must give in. The children may lose freedom in certain parts of the house. The husband may feel like a go-between for his wife and mother or mother-in-law. The issues of what should be expected and who makes certain decisions produce tensions. In the changed relationships individuals may feel they do not know where they stand or who they are. If the older couple is placed in facilities for the aged, they may feel completely deprived of identity, as though they are objects to be cared for rather than people.

Identity and Changing Circumstances

Changing circumstances can lead to an identity crisis at any point in life where a set of relationships and meanings change, regardless of whether the change is considered positive or negative. These are some examples of changing circumstances:

> leaving school and beginning a career
> getting married
> having a baby
> adopting a child
> getting a divorce
> moving to a different community
> losing a job
> getting a promotion
> losing a loved one
> suffering prolonged illness
> developing a physical handicap

Identity and Changing Values

Sometimes people feel they have lost their identity when they are completely out of tune with changing values. This is an experience similar to culture shock, when people try to adjust to a different set of customs and values. People feel they do not belong when their perceptions of what is acceptable and proper have changed drastically. For example, their children talk casually about sex and live in coed dorms at college. Their friends are divorced. Girls wear jeans to church. Attitudes toward abortion, crime, and ethical matters are all too confusing. They begin to question their own worth in such a changing world.

Identity and Self-Esteem

When the teacher understands the difference between secular and Christian concepts of identity and self, he can be most helpful to those who have identity problems. Non-Christian psychologists who write books and hold seminars on the subjects of identity and self-esteem are thinking of mankind without God. And without God mankind has only one basic motivation: self-gratification. Finding an identity, then, is a matter of being true to the pleasure principle—to get pleasure and avoid pain or discomfort. Life has no higher meaning. According to this viewpoint, good and intimate relationships can be established with other persons only if they do not require personal compromise.

We get trapped into thinking in terms of fancy words such as *positive self-esteem* and *self-worth,* and we forget that psychologists without God believe human beings are an accident of nature. All the excellent studies concerning the adaptations we should make to life and death come to one conclusion: If you really accept yourself you will learn to make the most of meaninglessness. To be healthy and normal is simply to love yourself and develop some personal interests that seem to please you. If you can form pleasant relationships with others without hindering the gratification of your own needs, then you should do so—since generally this leads to more satisfaction for everyone involved.

In contrast to this, Christians view man as God's highest creation, made by God in His own image and having significant meaning and purpose within His plan. But a strange paradox exists in the teachings of both secular psychologists and the church. Psychologists put high value on self-esteem and think of human beings as having unusual worth—even though they believe man is basically a biological accident. On the other hand, the church, believing in divine creation and purpose, generally puts more emphasis on the worthlessness of human beings. It seems sad that while the doctrines of Christianity emphasize the value of human souls for whom Christ paid with His own blood, many Christians teach people to feel inferior to keep them from the self-indulgence promoted by the secular world.

The best solution to this problem is for teachers to know what the Bible truly teaches about man and relay that fully and honestly, asking the Holy Spirit's guidance in making appropriate applications. A good first step is to help believers get their minds off themselves as individuals and think about their true purpose and relationship with God and with one another.

In the beautiful high priestly prayer of Christ (John 17) the highest of all affirmations is given human beings. Jesus makes it plain that God loves the disciples exactly as He loves His own Son! The same glory Christ brought to earth as God's representative was passed on to people just like us. There is even, according to one commentator, "a close correspondence between the mission of Jesus and the mission of the disciples." People are *that* loved and *that* important to God. And just as significant, if we are to understand our own worth and identity, God gives to human beings the materials out of which personal worth and identity are developed. These are the same materials mentioned by the psychologists: *somebody and something to be true to, meaning and purpose in life and a set of relationships.* For Christians, the meaning is the perpetuation of Christ's work and the set of relationships is the body of Christ.

Instead of placing emphasis on these truths, many ministers and teachers emphasize the fallen nature of man, using terms such as total depravity. Some sincere Christians believe there is nothing good in them. They accept the idea that they are like worms. They are afraid to express any positive evaluation of themselves, thinking that would be pride. They need to be taught that the difference between pride and healthy self-esteem is that pride is based on individual comparisons and competition with others. Pride includes the desire for personal recognition and the refusal to give sincere gratitude and credit to God and other people.

Self-esteem is an honest evaluation of personal worth, without comparison to others; acceptance of one's place of usefulness to others and the significance of one's contributions in the home, church, and workplace (cf. 2 Corinthians 10:12 and Romans 12:3-8). Humility does not mean self-condemnation and taking the blame in every situation. Rather, it means willingness to lift up other people and work as a team member without undue desire for personal credit.

What People Are Worth to God

In the true story of Billie the migrant girl whose life was

changed by an experience in Sunday school, the teacher helped her see herself as God sees children. She was not to think of herself as a dirty little fruitpicker who had no friends and could not read. She was not a nameless urchin in line at the welfare office.

"You are a child of God," the teacher said, forgetting all about the doctrine of total depravity as she reached out in love to a small human and granted her identity. "You are a child of God."[2]

To help people develop healthy self-esteem and identity, teachers must give them opportunities to think of themselves as the Bible describes them. Here is a list of such descriptions.

All human beings are
  made in God's image (Genesis 1:26,27)
  objects of His love and concern (1 John 4:9,10)
  souls for whom Christ died (Romans 3:23,24 and 1 Timothy 1:15,16)
  keepers of His earth, beneficiaries of His provision (Genesis 1:28-30; 9:2; Psalm 8:6-8)

All who believe in Christ are
  His treasured possession (Malachi 3:17)
  sheep of His pasture (Psalm 100:3)
  under His constant protection (Psalm 91)
  ransomed by the blood of Christ (Ephesians 1:7,8)
  fellow citizens with His people (Ephesians 2:19)
  friends of Jesus (John 15:13,14)
  joint heirs with Jesus (Romans 8:17)
  chosen to carry on the work of Jesus (Matthew 28:18-20)
  the temple of the Holy Spirit, God's building (1 Corinthians 6:19,20)
  the light of the world and the salt of the earth (Matthew 5:13-16)

Identity and Guilt

The term guilt has two major meanings with which Christian teachers should be familiar. First there is *true guilt,* which means actually being responsible for wrongdoing. A person who is guilty before God has failed to live up to his knowledge of God's laws and standards. In psychology this kind of guilt before God is not recognized. Therefore most attention is given to *guilt feelings,* which are feelings of falling short of one's ideals, causing some kind of trouble for which punishment should be expected, or blaming oneself in an irrational way.

The Christian teacher knows people need to feel guilty when true guilt is involved, for in this manner the conscience is formed. When a person feels guilty because of real sin, the problem can be solved only by sincere repentance and commitment to Christ.

Irrational guilt feelings result when people set up ideals or expectations for themselves and then cannot live up to them, or when they fail to understand what the Bible teaches about sin and forgiveness. Teachers can help their students realize they need a healthy, mature Christian conscience, but not a helpless, defeated attitude of constant guilt.

Children and the Development of Identity

For developing a person's sense of worth and identity, nothing can substitute for early teaching and parental example. Unhealthy guilt feelings can be prevented and an effective conscience established at home.

Teachers of parents must help them to understand the home climate shapes the child as nothing else can. This climate should be loving and forgiving, yet teaching principles of right and wrong. If the parents' attitudes are too rigid, demanding, condemning, blaming, and accusing, then fear and irrational guilt feelings will develop in the child. Parents must be consistent and realistic in their expectations.

Some Guidelines for Helping Children in Sunday School

Explain to children the meaning of what they are asked to do. Obedience just for the sake of obedience may lead to rebellion when no authority figure is present. When children see the reason for obedience, they can internalize the behavior and make it a part of their own identity. The child's favorite question ("Why?") reminds us of his need for meaning.

Never say to a child, "You are bad." Say, "You can do better. Do this instead of that." The child should learn that he will do some things that are wrong, but these can be changed and they do not mean he is a bad person.

Teach Bible stories of love and forgiveness. Strongly emphasize the need to forgive others. Then, when the child seeks salvation he will recognize his own need for forgiveness and be able to accept the forgiveness of God.

Never encourage competition or base evaluation of a child's performance on that of another child. Teach cooperation and teamwork.

Teach children to appreciate the contributions of others and to be thankful for what is done for them in the home, church, school, and community.

Summary

Gary Collins says, "There is no institution that comes even near to the biblical church in educating people toward a more positive self-concept."[3]

Biblical teaching and group dynamics are the best tools for helping people develop self-esteem and to cope with identity crises. The Sunday school teaches the basic principles of successful living and gives opportunities for positive relationships and meaningful activities.

Guide students away from the tendency to criticize and evaluate everything and everybody. Help them to discuss issues in honest but objective terms.

Encourage private Bible reading and meditation. The Scriptures actually become a part of the personal identity. "How sweet are your promises to my taste. . . . I gain understanding from your precepts" (Psalm 119:103,104). As we "eat" the Scriptures in study and meditation they nourish our personality and become a part of our spiritual person, just as food becomes a part of our physical body.

Emphasize forgiveness: Forgive people. Forgive yourself. Accept with gladness the forgiveness of God. Allow other people to forgive you; don't hang on to blame in order to feel humble.

Organize projects that require teamwork and cooperation.

Express appreciation for class members. Recognize personal achievements of all kinds: talents, such as musical ability, which are seen in public as well as achievements in the home, at work, in Christian service, and in the student's personal life. Be careful not to give too much attention to a few special talents or persons.

People sometimes come into the Sunday school class feeling like failures. Some are guilty and self-blaming because of events that happened during the week. Some have not lived up to their own expectations of themselves. Some think other people despise them. Some feel unfulfilled, pressed into roles or tasks that seem meaningless to them. Many of them are asking, "Who am I, really?"

The sensitive teacher smiles, opens the Bible, and says, "You are children of God."

NOTES

[1]Erik H. Erikson, *Identity, Youth and Crises* (New York: W. W. Norton and Company, Inc., 1968).

[2]Agnes McCarthy, Kenner Agnew, eds., *Prose and Poetry for Enjoyment* (Chicago: L. W. Singer Co., 1963).

[3]Gary R. Collins, *Christian Counseling* (Waco, TX: Word Books, 1980).